insight text guide

Tim Roberts

Of Mice and Men

John Steinbeck

insight®
▸innovative ▸engaging ▸evolving

First published in 2021, reprinted in 2023, 2024, 2025.

Insight Publications Pty Ltd
3/350 Charman Road
Cheltenham VIC 3192
Australia
Tel: +61 3 8571 4950
Email: books@insightpublications.com.au

www.insightpublications.com.au

A catalogue record for this book is available from the National Library of Australia

John Steinbeck's Of Mice and Men / Tim Roberts

Tim Roberts asserts the moral right to be identified as the author of this work.

ISBNs:
9781922525550 (print)
9781922525567 (digital)

Cover design by Gisela Beer

Printed by Markono Print Media Pte Ltd

contents

CHARACTER MAP

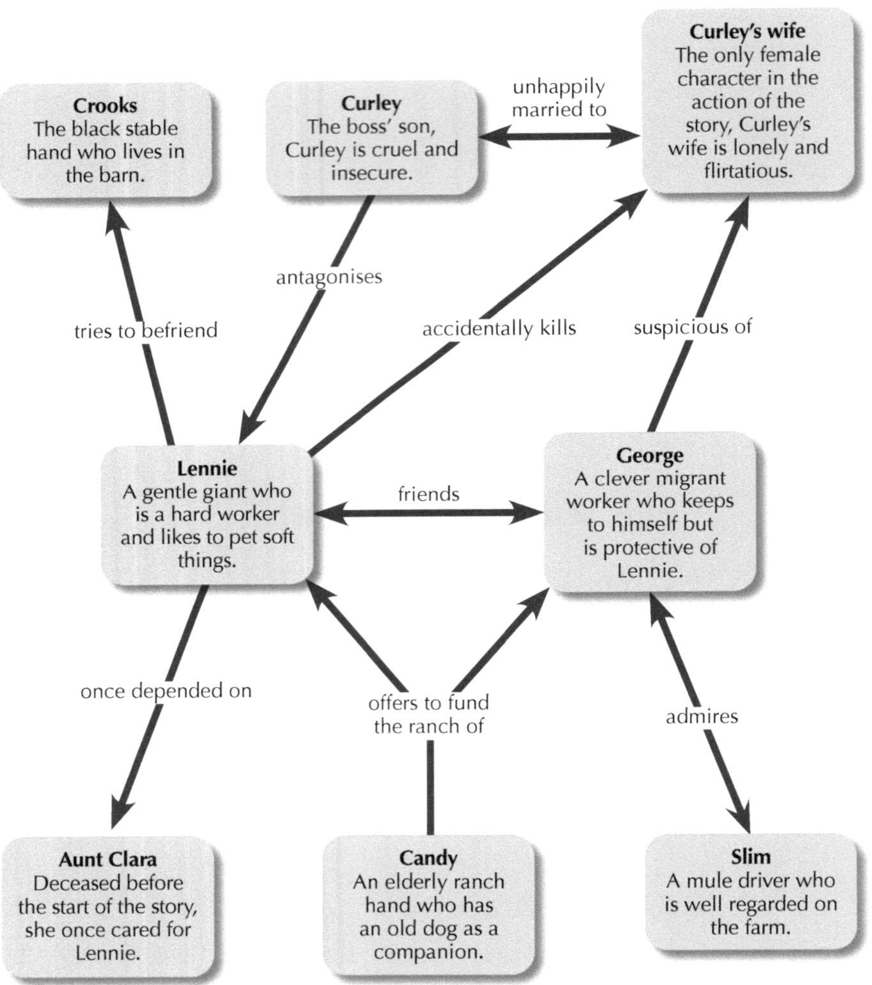

OVERVIEW

About the author

John Steinbeck (1902–1968) was an American novelist whose works dealt with the social and economic problems of rural labour. He attended Stanford University in the early 1920s but did not receive a degree, and he scraped together a living as an unskilled worker in California while writing. These vivid early experiences were central to his fiction, lending authenticity to the working-class characters in his stories.

Steinbeck had a relatively inauspicious (unpromising) start as a writer, with his first few novels failing to reach the popularity of his later works. It was not until 1935 that he found critical and commercial success with the novel *Tortilla Flat*, whose idyllic setting provided escapism for readers during the Great Depression of the 1930s. His subsequent novels were more serious in nature and more aggressive in their social criticism; for example, *In Dubious Battle* (1936) describes the brutal aftermath of a labour strike, while *Of Mice and Men* (1937), highly popular in Steinbeck's lifetime, details the struggles and lack of opportunities facing migrant workers.

In 1939, Steinbeck published what is considered his best work, *The Grapes of Wrath*, about a poor farming family that is driven from their home in Oklahoma by drought and economic hardship. After the runaway success of *The Grapes of Wrath*, Steinbeck never had to struggle financially again. However, his fiction retained his concern for workers and he was often regarded as a champion of the working class, at a time when sympathising with the poor was often viewed with suspicion.

Steinbeck's fiction often used language considered brutally frank for the time – including the sexist and racist slurs used by workers, unflinchingly displayed in *Of Mice and Men*. This commitment to realism stemmed from Steinbeck's left-wing politics, including the belief in improving conditions for the poor through government assistance.

(The US President when *Of Mice and Men* was published, Franklin Delano Roosevelt, was elected in 1933 on a promise to address the problems caused by the Great Depression through direct government assistance.)

Steinbeck was branded a socialist by many for his beliefs – a dangerous position in the early 1930s, when the prospect of the US becoming socialist seemed plausible. While Steinbeck sympathised with many socialist ideas, even joining the League of American Writers (often regarded as a communist organisation) in 1935, he was reluctant to make political commitments, regarding socialism as 'another form of religion' (Parini 1994).

Steinbeck's cultural importance was recognised when he was awarded the Nobel Prize for Literature in 1962 'for his realistic and imaginative writings, combining as they do sympathetic humour and keen social perception' (Nobel Committee).

Synopsis

The start of the novella introduces two travelling companions who are archetypal opposites: Lennie, who is huge, lumbering and intellectually disabled; and George, who is small, clever and hot-tempered. The two friends are on the road, having fled the town of Weed after a woman falsely accused Lennie of raping her. They are now making their way to a ranch near Soledad, California where they plan to work for a short time to save enough money to purchase a plot of land for themselves – a fantasy that sustains them through their hardships.

The two men arrive at the farmstead where they stay in squalid, cramped conditions. Almost immediately, they are confronted by the boss' son, Curley, who dislikes larger men and makes a point of targeting Lennie. Despite this, Lennie rapidly gains respect from his fellow workers for his work ethic and physical strength. He and George befriend Candy, an elderly ranch hand with an old sheepdog who is put down by fellow worker Carlson, and Slim, a confident and gentle mule herder whom the other workers hold in high regard. Slim, whose dog has recently given birth to a litter, gifts a puppy each to Lennie and Candy. When Candy hears of George and Lennie's plan to buy their own farm, he offers to pitch in $350 of his own money in exchange for being able to join them. George reluctantly agrees.

Curley's flirtatious wife, who is seen as a 'tramp' by the workers on the ranch, attracts Lennie, who lacks the restraint to tactfully conceal his desire. Sensing danger, George tells him to keep clear. Curley's insecurity about his wife eventually leads to conflict as he starts beating Lennie. After avoiding violence for as long as possible, Lennie finally retaliates by injuring Curley's hand.

When George leaves Lennie to go to the town brothel with the other workers, Lennie visits the barn housing Crooks, a black man ostracised by the other workers. After hearing of Lennie and George's dream, Crooks offers to join them in exchange for his board. Candy finds them and they discuss the plan further. Curley's wife enters the barn and flirts with the men before Candy tells her off.

The next day, while the other workers are playing horseshoes outside, Lennie accidentally kills his puppy in the barn. Curley's wife enters and takes the opportunity to talk with Lennie alone, telling him about her unhappiness being married to Curley and her failed dreams of being a movie star. She offers to let Lennie stroke her hair but panics when he holds on too tight, causing her to scream. This frightens Lennie, who unintentionally breaks her neck, killing her instantly. He flees, to the place in the clearing previously agreed upon with George.

Candy finds Curley's wife's body and runs to get George. When the other workers find out, they form a lynch mob intent on exacting revenge and murdering Lennie. Realising what this means for achieving his dream, George resolves to kill Lennie before the other farmhands reach him. He finds Lennie by the river, speaking in his imagination with his deceased Aunt Clara, who cared for him as a boy. Lennie asks George to relate their shared dream, which he does one final time before shooting him.

Character summaries

George Milton

George is a travelling ranch worker who keeps his sights set on a better life. His rough manners and appearance are in keeping with the other ranch workers. As a physically small man, George seems diminutive compared to his travelling companion, Lennie.

Lennie Small

A large man with significant intellectual disabilities, Lennie is a loyal companion to George. He is inspired by the fantasy life George creates for them and obeys his friend's commands without question. After accidentally killing Curley's wife, he is shot by George before the other ranch workers get to him.

Candy

Candy is an elderly ranch hand who offers to join George and Lennie in their plan to purchase a piece of land and settle down. He owns a similarly old and disabled dog who the other workers despise because of its smell.

Crooks

Crooks is an African-American stable hand who is excluded by the other people working on the farm. He lives alone in the stables, away from the other workers, and largely keeps to himself.

Slim

A highly skilled mule driver who works on the ranch, Slim is a quiet, insightful man who is well regarded by his fellow workers. The other men often look to Slim for advice, and he is shown to have compassion for other people and a level of understanding that the other workers on the farm lack.

Curley

The son of the ranch owner, Curley is a resentful, insecure and aggressive man who is easily threatened by others. A former lightweight boxer, he provokes and fights bigger men, such as Lennie, to demonstrate his strength. Though he often worries that his new wife is flirting with other men on the ranch, he exhibits little love for or appreciation of her.

Curley's wife

The only female character in the story, Curley's wife appears scandalously, carelessly seductive, which leads the workers at the ranch to view her as a 'tramp'. Unnamed throughout the story and left lonely and unfulfilled by her new husband, her backstory – about her broken dreams of being an actor – helps to portray her in a more sympathetic light.

Carlson

An unfeeling mechanic on the ranch, Carlson bullies Candy into putting down his dog. He is a narrowly pragmatic and materialistic man who lacks empathy, failing to understand how a dog can bring comfort to an old man.

Aunt Clara

The deceased Aunt Clara is the original link between George and Lennie. Having raised Lennie after he was abandoned by his mother, she is a benevolent presence throughout the story, and appears to Lennie in the final moments before his death.

BACKGROUND & CONTEXT

Historical setting

The novella is set in the rich agricultural region of California encompassing Soledad and Salinas during the Great Depression. Steinbeck was keenly aware of the many conflicts and paradoxes of this environment – workers laboured in a verdant paradise, yet couldn't even manage to raise enough funds to support themselves, let alone improve their situation. It was a vision of scarcity among plenty.

California's Salinas Valley was seen as providing incomparable opportunities for workers in the 1930s, due to its incredible fertility. However, the hands-off policies of the government, led by President Herbert Hoover, were seen as insufficiently compassionate towards the farmers themselves. The poverty and deprivation that the labourers are confronted with in the novella can be seen as a direct criticism of the then-government's unfeeling policy towards people who worked on the land during the Great Depression.

The Great Depression was exacerbated in the US by a catastrophic series of droughts, beginning in 1930 and commonly referred to as the Dust Bowl. Coupled with the depressed American economy, these natural disasters caused great hardship and suffering for agricultural workers. In *The Grapes of Wrath*, Steinbeck wrote about how the extended drought in the Plains region forced tens of thousands of migrants to move to California to avoid starvation. As with its response to the Great Depression, Hoover's government was seen as inadequately compassionate towards those whose lives had been destroyed.

The Great Depression and the Dust Bowl were decisive events that caused America to turn away from unchecked capitalism – notably in the agricultural industry – and towards a more heavily regulated system monitored by government. President Franklin Delano Roosevelt was instrumental in creating a closer relationship between farmers and government; his approach starkly contrasted with his predecessor,

Herbert Hoover, who believed in collective self-help as a remedy for poverty.

Author's context

Steinbeck was a prolific author whose works are linked by a concern for the working class. While he came from a fairly affluent background, he was consistently involved in addressing workers' struggles through his fiction. Most importantly, like Lennie and George, Steinbeck worked as a so-called 'bindle-stiff' (a travelling labourer who carries their belongings over their shoulder) in California in the late 1920s. This experience gave him the firsthand knowledge to write authentically from working people's perspectives, a trait for which his writing has received wide acclaim.

Publishing context/history

While *Of Mice and Men* was immediately successful upon publication, it has since been banned in several US public and school libraries for allegedly being derogatory towards African Americans, women and the developmentally disabled. In particular, it has been challenged for its use of racial epithets (insults) to describe the stable hand, Crooks, which some educators suggest causes unnecessary offence to students of colour.

Although *Of Mice and Men* has been proposed for censorship more than fifty times since its release and appeared on numerous Top 100 Most Banned and Challenged Books lists (compiled by the American Library Association), many people have argued that, due to its literary merit, it should be protected. Furthermore, in defending this book, many critics and scholars have pointed to the difference between the *author's* intentions and the *characters'* own voices within the text. For example, Steinbeck's commitment to representing racism in his novella was made with an explicit goal of condemning the racist attitude of his characters – not condoning it. The use of harsh and upsetting language was seen by Steinbeck as necessary to make the wider point about how racism dehumanises people and corrupts their morals.

GENRE, STRUCTURE & LANGUAGE

Genre

Of Mice and Men is regarded as a primarily realist piece of fiction, written in a dialogue-heavy manner with few adornments. In the introduction to the Penguin edition, Susan Shillinglaw states that Steinbeck wrote many of his works to be accurately represented on stage, with the confined settings and stripped-back nature of the descriptions in *Of Mice and Men* reflecting this judgement.

While *Of Mice and Men* focuses on depicting the real-world experiences of its characters, there are also elements of other genres (discussed hereafter) that are evident in Steinbeck's work.

Pastoral literature

In one sense, the novella *Of Mice and Men* is part of a long American literary tradition idealising rural life. This theme, of course, has a long history that stretches back to antiquity – for example, the Roman poet Virgil's *Eclogues*, a series of poems dramatising farming life.

Many of Steinbeck's natural descriptions resemble American nature poets such as Robert Frost:

> My long two-pointed ladder's sticking through a tree
> Toward heaven still,
> And there's a barrel that I didn't fill
> Beside it, and there may be two or three
> Apples I didn't pick upon some bough.
> (*After Apple-Picking*, 1914)

While works belonging to the pastoral genre traditionally show a more optimistic view of the country lifestyle, Steinbeck uses the beauty of his setting to make darker, more pessimistic points about the supposedly simplistic and undefiled nature of rural living.

The social problem novel

Of Mice and Men contains elements of what is referred to as the 'social problem novel', in which a prevailing social problem is explored through its effect on the characters of a work of fiction.

Steinbeck was one of a group of writers in the early- to mid-twentieth century who resolved to chronicle life *as it was*, without being unnecessarily mannered or removed from ordinary people's everyday reality. Yet unlike the more committed writers in the group, most notably Sinclair Lewis, Steinbeck's hard-hitting dramatisations of ordinary people's speech and behaviour are always coupled with a romantic sensibility that stood in opposition to his commitment to realism.

Steinbeck was highly committed to representing realistic behaviour on a descriptive level – for example, the descriptions of the humid atmosphere of the barn where Crook is confined, the squalid quarters of the farmers, and other convincing details of deprivation that people suffered during the Great Depression. However, he was not so concerned with offering a large collection of detail about this life for scene-setting purposes. Every word of the characters' dialogue advances the plot, which always remains the central focus. Steinbeck was not interested in providing the reader with a type of documentary narrative, full of detailed descriptions of farm conditions. Instead, he was much more concerned with the fate of the characters within this world.

The anti-morality play

There is a clear religious sensibility informing the novella's seemingly normal events. Lennie and George's trajectory starts out as a stirring rags-to-riches story, even though the riches both men desire are comparatively modest. While neither man is perfect, they both have good hearts and could be seen to 'deserve' a life of happiness. In a more traditional story of redemption, their good intentions would eventually bring them earthly rewards, in contrast to the fallen figures surrounding them.

However, this is not the lesson we get from *Of Mice and Men*. The religious force that would have provided George and Lennie with the happy ending they deserved is absent; instead, the world of the novella doesn't seem to offer a genuine possibility of justice or redemption for its characters.

The forces in control of the novella's world, then, don't necessarily correspond to religious ones. The world of George and Lennie seems to be godless, with any greater meaning that the characters believe in dismissed as illusory. The character arc of redemption that a more traditional narrative would provide is simply absent; there is nobody pulling the strings for these characters behind the scenes, as they end up broken, disappointed and destroyed.

Romanticism

Steinbeck has often been seen as a Romantic writer, particularly in his earlier works. The Romantic movement is notable for its insistence that our current world is 'fallen', as it harks back to an earlier age that we have lost. Many Romantic narratives tell the story of attempting to regain the perfect world that we have lost. This Romantic idea of a lost Golden Age is based on a Greek idea, which saw the current time as a corrupted Iron Age in comparison. It also has clear parallels with the Garden of Eden myth, which tells the story of how Adam and Eve were expelled from the garden and condemned to wander the earth.

While this idea of recovering a lost world is appealing, it obviously poses problems for realist fiction. Romanticism has been criticised for a failure to engage with real-life problems in favour of fantasy solutions, a charge that the Romantically inclined Steinbeck often faced. Yet he seems intensely sceptical about the possibility of reaching paradise in *Of Mice and Men*, which seems to heavily criticise the idea of a Golden Age. In Steinbeck's view, we must strive to make our current situation better with the tools available to us, rather than dreaming of travelling to a non-existent vision of paradise.

Structure

Although the novella has a simple plot with few events, several structural devices are used that complicate how the action unfolds.

Narrative structure

As a novella, *Of Mice and Men* employs a fairly simple narrative structure; it is divided into six sections, as detailed below.

- Section 1 (pp.3–18) covers George and Lennie's trek to the farmstead.
- Section 2 (pp.19–38) introduces most of the second-order characters who work or live on the farm.
- Section 3 (pp.39–65) details George and Lennie's first days on the job, culminating in Lennie's fight with Curley.
- Section 4 (pp.66–82) takes place in the barn where Crooks lives, and details conversations between him, Lennie, Candy and Curley's wife.
- Section 5 (pp.83–97), which can be seen as the novella's climax, begins with the death of Lennie's pup and ends with Lennie fleeing the farm after accidentally killing Curley's wife.
- Section 6 (pp.98–106) covers the fatal resolution of the novella, in which George finds Lennie in the clearing where they agreed to meet in case of trouble and kills him before the other workers find him.

The first and last sections are set outdoors, while the middle four sections are set in the farm's interior – Sections 2 and 3 in the bunkhouse, and Sections 4 and 5 in the barn. The neatness of this structure enables Steinbeck to present his story in a tightly compressed form.

However, the tale is complicated by Steinbeck's frequent venturing out of this narrow time scheme in order to provide us with more information about Lennie and George, which he does through flashbacks.

The primary role of the flashback sequences is to fill in more information about these two people's lives. For that reason, we learn about Lennie and George's past – for example, the events in the town of Weed (pp.8–13). The relevant information about this episode is revealed gradually by George, interrupted by the two men's efforts to settle down for the night. The second-hand way more information about the characters is revealed mimics everyday life.

The story also includes potted biographies (just the main facts of someone's life) of the other characters told in flashback. The most significant of these belongs to Candy, who laments his precarious situation:

> 'I got hurt four years ago,' he said. 'They'll can me purty soon. Jus' as soon as I can't swamp out no bunk houses they'll put me on the county ... When they can me here I wisht somebody'd shoot me. But they won't do nothing like that.' (p.60)

We receive similar backstories for Crooks (p.70) and Curley's wife (pp.86–7), which fosters empathy for these downtrodden, forgotten, neglected and misunderstood characters.

Foreshadowing

One of the main structuring devices used by Steinbeck is called foreshadowing – that is, providing information that will become important later in the novella, both to create tension and to encourage the reader to view earlier events in a different, more nuanced light.

One example is the repeated references to something terrible happening in the previous town George and Lennie worked in. As we are given more and more information about what occurred there, a sense of foreboding develops that a similar thing could happen again:

> 'You crazy son-of-a-bitch. You keep me in hot water all the time.' He took on the elaborate manner of little girls when they are mimicking each other. 'Jus' wanted to feel that girl's dress – jus' wanted to pet it like it was a mouse – Well, how the hell did she know you jus' wanted to feel her dress? She jerks back and you hold on like it was a mouse.' (p.13)

When the penultimate chapter opens with the ominous image of 'the four-taloned Jackson fork suspended from its pulley' (p.83), the mood darkens. We have been prepared for a rerun of the Weed incident; the dread soon begins as we are presented with the image of 'a little dead puppy that lay in front of [Lennie]' (p.83). The undisciplined energy that Lennie has displayed throughout is now a genuine danger – except this time, George is not here to rescue him.

The most obvious act of foreshadowing is Lennie's constant overenthusiastic petting of animals, which escalates until the climax of the novella, when Lennie accidentally kills Curley's wife (p.90). With the animals, as well as with the two women, Lennie's violence is made more disturbing by the fact that it is caused by excessive, childish affection. The dead mouse that Lennie tries to conceal at the outset (p.10), the puppy he prematurely removes from the nest (p.43) and the dead puppy revealed in the barn (p.83) all demonstrate Lennie's inability to manifest his emotions safely. As each example of Lennie's past attentions is revealed to the reader, the expectation steadily builds that something terrible will happen again. Foreshadowing therefore builds tension in *Of Mice and Men*, without dissipating until the climax of the second-last scene.

The play-within-a-play

The recurring dream of the farm with rabbits, of which Lennie and George fondly speak, is brought up so often it effectively becomes a parallel story, coexisting with the present-day one. Each time the story is told, it undergoes subtle variations and shifts in tone; even the sceptical George is emotionally affected by it. Even though the story subtly changes depending on who is telling it, with Lennie chiming in at different times and George often changing minor details, there is a sacred sense of stability to this shared vision of the future, protected from the precarious nature of the men's lives.

The vision of owning this piece of land is so intoxicating that, when the other men are drawn into its orbit, they seek to inhabit the same sense of peace and sanctified goodness that George and Lennie can access. Even when they are seemingly in reach of securing their dream, the farm always seems like an impossible goal in a fallen world.

The fable

A fable is a moral tale, whose narrative serves to deliver its message at its conclusion. All other aims of the story are subordinated to the goal of conveying this message to the reader.

Of Mice and Men contains many elements of the fable. The highly compressed description, the lack of extraneous detail and the moral clarity of the conclusion all point to a fable-like narrative. There are virtually no wasted words in the form of detailed description in the novella; apart from a few self-contained interludes at the beginnings of sections (e.g. p.3, p.66, p.83), we are given the bare minimum required to picture the action.

Instead, the fates of the characters and their moral predicaments dominate. In *Of Mice and Men* Steinbeck argues against the idea that people are rewarded for being good and just; instead, he implies that there is no moral organising principle of the universe that ensures they are all looked after – there is simply the reality in which they exist now. Because of this, characters such as George and Lennie must do all they can to alter their circumstances. This can only be achieved by force, because it will be resisted at every turn by those in power.

The moral of this fable can be compared to that of the poem by Scottish poet Robert Burns from which the title *Of Mice and Men* derives. Writing in Scots dialect in his poem 'To a Mouse', Burns tells of the futility of making plans in an indifferent world:

> The best laid schemes o' Mice an' Men
> Gang aft agley,
> An' lea'e us nought but grief an' pain,
> For promis'd joy!

The line 'Gang aft agley' means 'often go wrong'. Burns is therefore explaining that trying to plan one's own life while ignoring the universe's greater plans is futile; as creatures with limited comprehension of our world, we are forever doomed to be at the mercy of greater forces that we don't fully comprehend.

Burns' melancholic poem mirrors a similar sentiment in Gloucester's bitter lines (from Shakespeare's *King Lear*) about the fragility of maintaining our hopes in the face of a cruel universe:

> As flies to wanton boys are we to the gods;
> They kill us for their sport. (Act 4, Scene 1)

Language

Dialogue

Steinbeck is known for his claim that he wished to represent people as they really were in life. The raw, uncensored feel to the men's dialogue in this novella was quite scandalous for the time; certain sections remain so today – notably the vile racial slurs habitually used by others against Crooks, as well as some of the men's talk about women (including derogatory terms such as 'jail bait').

While it is often overlooked in more high-minded criticism, slang is just as essential in Steinbeck's rhetorical world; in fact, his unique authorial voice would be unrecognisable without it. The creative and interesting informal terms used by the men are key to their personalities, providing an insight into the way this neglected class of people used language in their everyday lives. As a mode of speaking that has been long devalued by the elite class, slang is cherished by Steinbeck as an individual mode of expression that has been unfairly dismissed by those in power to keep disadvantaged people down.

This may not seem like a novel idea to us, because we have grown up listening to slang terms on TV and reading them in books, but, in the 1930s, the division between literary and everyday language was much stricter. Including slang in a realistic story without subtly denigrating (dismissing) it was seen as quite a radical move for an ambitious novelist such as Steinbeck. This appreciation of slang has much in common with modern views of dialects as equally valid ways of speaking. For example, the dialect of a farmer working on a remote cattle station is no longer seen as inferior to the dialect used by an investment banker; instead, it is valued as a different mode of expression. Steinbeck was one of the authors who contributed to our changed view of the English language and its various forms.

Poetic description

Contrasting with the earthy slang used by the men is Steinbeck's awareness of natural beauty, which is evident in his sparing yet poetic descriptions of nature. Even when depressing or traumatic moments lurk on the following page, Steinbeck will occasionally make space to include a meditative moment on natural beauty. Consider the passage below from the opening of the novella.

> On the sandy bank under the trees the leaves lie deep and so crisp that a lizard makes a great skittering if he runs among them. Rabbits come out of the brush to sit on the sand in the evening, and the damp flats are covered with the night tracks of 'coons, and with the spread pads of dogs from the ranches, and with the split-wedge tracks of deer that come to drink in the dark. (p.3)

This type of description does not advance the plot, provide us with more information about the characters or otherwise add to the narrative. It is the type of thick description that is absent inside the farmstead; the loving attention that Steinbeck pays to the woods surrounding the farm implicitly positions the farm itself as a break in the natural world. This meditative space seems to hold mysteries beyond Lennie and George's comprehension, which is echoed in the promise of their imagined homestead.

The authorial personality

Steinbeck seems to take a hands-off approach to his characters; he describes what they do without offering us asides about what he thinks about them. As such, the reader witnesses events as if they are hearing dialogue in a play.

When Steinbeck talked about his fictional works, he strove to sustain the illusion that his characters were unfolding organically, with him simply standing back. This technique is known as showing rather than telling.

This hands-off approach is, of course, an illusion. Steinbeck has created and structured the entire work and supplied all the detail we read on each page. Even though we don't hear his overt views on the events that unfold (as we would from a nineteenth-century author such as Dickens), Steinbeck is still in full control of his message. Unlike in his more expansive novels, though, *Of Mice and Men*'s style is extremely sparse.

SECTION-BY-SECTION ANALYSIS

Section 1 (pp.3–18)

Summary: *The two main characters, George and Lennie, are introduced at a campsite, sharing their vision of an idyllic future before having to begin their hard lives at the next farm.*

The novella begins 'a few miles south of Soledad' (p.3), in a fictional rural location in California based on Salinas. Two migrant workers, George and Lennie, refresh themselves with food and drink before camping for the night. In the slang of the day, they are bindle-stiffs. The sparseness of their possessions marks them as impoverished.

The two men are described as opposites – Lennie huge and lumbering, George 'small and quick' (p.4). It is soon apparent that Lennie has an intellectual disability, with George acting as his sole carer. Lennie looks to George as a small child would their father. His behaviour is often compared to an animal's – for example, 'snorting into the water like a horse' (p.4) and 'dabbl[ing] his big paw in the water' (p.5). George models behaviour for Lennie to follow, and often scolds Lennie for his transgressions – for example, holding a dead mouse (p.7, p.10). George grumpily snaps at Lennie, emphasising that he shouldn't talk to anyone, so as to avoid getting in trouble.

The idyllic moment that the two men are currently enjoying is skilfully contrasted with the strenuous future they face. Relaxing, George declares, 'tonight I'm gonna lay right here and look up. I like it' (p.9). Reflecting his working-class concerns, Steinbeck shows people of humble means experiencing modest moments of joy.

Another carefully balanced contrast established in this opening section is George's love-hate relationship with Lennie. Lennie's request for ketchup on his beans sends George over the edge, as he furiously yells that 'whatever we ain't got, that's what you want' (p.12). Yet just a few seconds later, George is wracked with guilt when he sees 'Lennie's anguished face' (p.13). This teetering between love and hate is an ever-present dynamic in his and Lennie's relationship.

The pair's supper foreshadows the novella's tragic end, as George resentfully reminds Lennie that 'you do bad things and I got to get you out' (p.13), a dark note echoed by George's sombre advice to 'hide in the brush' (p.17) and wait if disaster strikes. As this suggests, George knows from the outset that their careful plan could fall apart. By raising this suggestion, Steinbeck uses this first scene to generate suspense; there is the understanding that something bad could happen at any moment.

As Lennie and George butt heads about trivialities, the contours of this odd couple's relationship emerge. Whereas George is brusque and dismissive, Lennie is childlike and dependent, his touching vulnerability making his threat to 'go off in the hills an' find a cave' (p.14) sound like a small child threatening to leave home.

George's first recounting of their imagined future on the ranch introduces their rich fantasy lives, woven through every subsequent scene. George is as deeply invested as Lennie, as he repeats his words 'rhythmically as though he had said them many times before' (p.15). The mantra of escape soothes both men, supplying them with a bountiful future that outshines their impoverished present.

George is clearly aware that he could have led another, more conventionally satisfying life without Lennie. Yet he can't commit to leaving, always stepping back from the brink. George's behaviour pattern of threat/remorse plays out repeatedly – for example, when he looks 'ashamedly at the flames' after 'Lennie's face was drawn with terror' (p.13). Every remark of George's must be carefully weighed for its potential effects on Lennie, who has little emotional control.

Key point

A crucial theme established in this opening scene that echoes through the novella is Lennie's undisciplined affection for animals. His regret that he 'pinched [the mice's] heads a little and then they was dead' (p.11) will spill over into his tragic killing of Curley's wife later in the story.

Key vocabulary

Cat house: a brothel.

Loo-loo: a 'look' at an attractive woman.

Stake: the deposit needed for a piece of land.

Q How does Lennie attempt to push back against George's control?

Q What are your first impressions of George and Lennie and the relationship they share?

Section 2 (pp.19–38)

Summary: *The two men have an inauspicious (unpromising) introduction to the farm. The gloomy tone is set by George's discovery of a can of insecticide in his bed. In the squalid bunkhouse, George and Lennie meet most of the other pivotal characters.*

The father/son dynamic established between George and Lennie in the first section intensifies here, as Lennie painstakingly echoes George's movements like a small boy imitating his father: 'George lifted his tick and looked underneath it. He leaned over and inspected the sacking closely. Immediately Lennie got up and did the same with his bed (p.21).

The gesture of copying is touching, but it also intensifies the danger Lennie is in. His attempts to present himself as a model employee fail; even as he amply displays his work ethic, his vulnerability marks him for disaster in this unforgiving environment. While Lennie is lucky to have George, there are few others with George's depth of compassion.

Nearly all gestures of friendship between the workers at the ranch are contaminated with cynicism and self-interest. The mood inside the bunkhouse is an unsettling mixture of camaraderie and underlying menace. In an attempted welcome, for example, Candy regales George with a grimly unfunny story about a fight between the previous skinner, Smitty, and the black stable hand, Crooks (p.22). Violence, clearly, is seen as trivial entertainment without moral importance.

The labouring lifestyle also corrodes human decency. A good example of the toll that a brutal life can have on a person is Carlson, a cynical, unimaginative and down-to-earth character with a streak of nastiness. Carlson spends much of the chapter convincing Candy to kill his old dog; while this is presented by Carlson as a mercy killing, his insistence on the deed seems gratuitous (over-the-top).

There is one exception to the sea of degradation on the farm: Slim, the novella's only unambiguously virtuous character. He is Curley's physical and moral opposite – strong, tall, hardworking, gentle and kind. In some ways, he is more of an archetype than a fully rounded character, described as almost godlike in his ability to see the truth. He is proof, then, that the decency of the common man can survive repeated assaults.

This section contains Steinbeck's most piercing criticisms of the human cost of exploitative labour, exemplified through the character of Candy. Candy has been severely injured on the job, and has been demoted to cleaning duties while living in fear of being 'canned' after losing his right hand in a work accident. Candy represents the struggles of 'the little guy' to stay afloat in an unsympathetic world.

The dominant side of labour is also heavily criticised. The entrance of the boss – a man portrayed as decidedly unimpressive – critiques the idea of meritocracy (the notion that talented and deserving people rise to the top). The boss' anticlimactic entrance reveals him as 'a little stocky man' with 'high-heeled boots and spurs to prove he was not a laboring man' (p.22). The boss is angry, suspicious and intentionally mediocre; though undeserving, he wields great power.

Steinbeck's criticism of the exploitation of farm labourers intensifies with the introduction to the despicable character of Curley. Even more than his father, the boss, Curley embodies oppression and nepotism (family-based favouritism). An insecure, aggressive man who's 'done quite a bit in the [boxing] ring' (p.27), Curley is a coward who knows he is protected by privilege. His hostility towards Lennie simply because he 'hates big guys' (p.28) is merely another example of his toxic personality.

Curley also represents the misogyny and sexism running through the novella. This is symbolised by his deep distrust of his wife around other men, a judgement many of the labourers share; for example, Candy bluntly describes her as 'a tart' (p.29). Even in such a hostile atmosphere, the issue of women's untrustworthiness is something on which the men agree. There are limits, then, to Steinbeck's empathy with these people, who blame women instead of unjust economic systems for their woes. This uneasy combination of female untrustworthiness and male control hovers over the story.

Key point

The character of Curley's wife shows Steinbeck's ambivalence towards women. While the novella criticises the men's more extreme pronouncements about her, she is still seen as a temptress who poses a threat to virtually all the men with whom she interacts.

Key vocabulary

Buck: a dismissive term for a black male.

Burlap: a rough fabric, like hessian.

Canned: fired.

Grayback/pants rabbit: a tick or louse.

Jerkline skinner: the person in charge of driving (herding) a team of mules.

Slang: gave birth to (pups).

Swamper: janitor.

Q How is Slim characterised differently from the other men?

Section 3 (pp.39–65)

Summary: *The sense of dread from the previous section intensifies, with various characters' suffering laid bare. The old, vulnerable Candy is revealed as a potential saviour for George and Lennie when he offers to fund their dream. Curley causes anxiety in others throughout this section, which steadily builds towards a brutal confrontation with Lennie.*

Aside from Lennie and George's shared dream of the farm, the only other source of hope in the novella is the burgeoning friendship between George and Slim. Slim's sincere and trustworthy nature allows George to open up to him about his and Lennie's past – something that the ultra-guarded George would not be comfortable revealing to others. There is some hope, then, for human relationships amid this unpromising environment.

George tells Slim about the death of Lennie's Aunt Clara and Lennie's subsequent life with him (p.40). The fact that George took Lennie in for compassionate reasons elicits respect from Slim. The quiet affinity between George and Slim brings out the similarities in their personalities, including Slim's appreciation of George's kindness. The two men seem to understand the potential for cruelty, and the importance of avoiding such behaviour where possible. Slim laments that 'ever'body in the whole damn world is scared of each other' (p.36), while George restores his faith by revealing that after having treated Lennie cruelly, 'I ain't done nothing like that no more' (p.41). George's changed outlook highlights that morally admirable behaviour, while difficult, is still possible in this unpromising world.

As so often in this novella, a small scene of tenderness is abruptly broken. Here, the conversation between George and Slim ceases when it is revealed that Lennie has brought in the pup that Slim gifted him, despite being far too young to leave its mother. It is another example of Lennie's overbearing affection endangering others, an admirable trait that ultimately dooms him.

The rest of the section is dominated by the pressure faced by Candy to kill his dog. Even Slim agrees, justifying this by stating: 'I wisht somebody'd shoot me if I got old an' a cripple' (p.46). This plotline contains an uneasy blend of compassion and violence, as Carlson's eagerness to kill the dog seems motivated by less than honourable impulses. Even Slim's support of the killing doesn't remove the scene's dark implications.

Sometimes, Steinbeck suggests, the need for companionship trumps more rational considerations. There is also an echo of George's relationship with Lennie in Candy's stubborn love of a dog who burdens him. Although affection is not always rational, Steinbeck considers it vital to our humanity.

Another central theme is the men's attitudes towards women. Even though George is not above sexist comments, he refuses to join in the other men's gleefully derogatory comments, only wryly observing that 'she's gonna make a mess' (p.52).

There are limits to George's more enlightened attitudes. When he is invited to a brothel in town, he declines because of the cost. Even when refusing to follow the other men in their pursuit of Curley's wife, George remains deeply suspicious of women's potential to destabilise and distract men from their purpose. He prefers prostitutes to relationships because 'a guy can go in an' get drunk and get ever'thing outta his system all at once, an' no messes' (p.56). While less harsh than the other men's views, it is nevertheless a deeply limited perspective of women as subordinate.

Again, Steinbeck engages in a play of contrasts between bleakness and hope. The turning point occurs when George and Lennie's discussion of their idealised future is overheard by Candy. As someone who has been beaten down by the system, he is attracted to the sanctuary promised by George – even offering to contribute 'three hunderd an' fifty bucks' (p.59) in exchange for being included. Just as the hope of friendship is briefly kindled by George and Slim's earlier conversation, Candy's offer presents a realistic means of achieving the men's dream.

This brief respite is abruptly punctured yet again – this time by Slim and Curley's re-entrance, with Slim angrily denying being interested in

Curley's wife. Seeking someone to antagonise, Curley challenges Lennie to a fight – with disastrous consequences as Lennie maims him in self-defence.

Key point

As with several other incidents in *Of Mice and Men*, a conflict over women disrupts a potentially hopeful moment between men.

Key vocabulary

Goo-goos: government reformers (short for 'good government guys').

Hoosegow: jail (a corruption of the Spanish 'juzgado', meaning 'panel of judges').

Q How does the novella undermine George's sense of hope for the future?

Section 4 (pp.66–82)

Summary: *The focus switches to Crooks, who has been largely excluded until this point. In the barn where he lives, Crooks is joined by Lennie, then Candy, then Curley's wife.*

After fleeting mentions of Crooks, the African-American stable hand, in previous sections, he makes a proper entrance in this section. The character of Crooks introduces an interesting dynamic: no matter how downtrodden the farm workers are, Crooks fares worse. In a world full of exploited people, he is an overlooked victim. It is to Steinbeck's credit that he dramatises Crooks' perspective.

Steinbeck draws the lines of Crooks' character extremely efficiently, showing how he clings to his intellectual ambitions even when given absolutely no opportunity to use them. A common thread emerges here: the resilience of human ambition and dignity in a cold and unpromising world. This theme of resilience and self-respect is reiterated when Crooks reacts with anger to Lennie entering his 'home'. Even though the space Crooks inhabits is just a squalid stable, he treats it with pride.

The confrontation between Crooks and Lennie continues Steinbeck's interest in the downtrodden. Here, two highly disadvantaged members of society – an intellectual disabled white man and an economically disadvantaged black man – meet on equal terms. Society has failed both men, with the consequences of their isolation and disadvantage laid bare.

Steinbeck's empathy for Crooks is evident in his decision to dedicate two full pages to Crook's solitary life (pp.66–7). After Lennie's intrusion into the barn, Crooks tries to flex his intellectual superiority by mocking Lennie's plans and making him fret over George's safety. This man, who has never had the chance to be anything other than exploited, is not above doing the same to others when the chance arises.

Yet this cynical perspective does not last. Sensing Lennie's harmlessness, Crooks gradually warms to him, even sharing the story of his early life (p.70). In these brief moments, we are shown the possibility of companionship between two men who have been rejected by society. Crooks is emotionally conflicted throughout the scene between feeling contempt for Lennie and craving his company.

The less honourable aspects of Crooks' attitude towards Lennie are quickly abandoned, as Lennie becomes distraught at Crooks' insinuations. It is apparent that as Crooks has nobody to talk to, he is simply sharing his loneliness.

The novella's signature mood – the rapid shift between hope and despair – is again displayed as Lennie shares the story of the farm that he, George and Candy are close to securing. To conceal the fact that he is attracted to the plan, Crooks cynically remarks that 'nobody never gets to heaven, and nobody gets no land' (p.73).

Yet this pessimistic note fails to extinguish the hope that has been building, even after Candy enters the barn. Such is his craving for company that it is 'difficult for Crooks to conceal his pleasure with anger' (p.74). The scene with the three men in the barn together, each daring to hope for a better life, is intensely optimistic. When Crooks realises the trio are close to having the money, he confesses in wonder that he has 'never seen a guy really do it' (p.76).

Yet again, a woman disrupts these best-laid plans. With the entrance of Curley's wife, the hope that has been quietly building is instantly destroyed. While the impressionable Lennie is entranced by her beauty, Crooks and Candy find themselves 'scowling down away from her eyes' (p.76).

Among the company of three subordinate men, Curley's wife tactlessly voices her dissatisfaction with her husband. Her decision to tell the story of her betrayal by a man who 'tol' me he could put me in pitchers' (p.78) shows that she, too, is vulnerable.

This fragile solidarity between the three men cannot stretch to accommodate this 'dangerous' woman. Instead of this moment being used to draw the woman into the shared story of exploitation and resilience, the men close ranks to exclude her:

> You don't know that we got our own ranch to go to, an' our own house. We ain't got to stay here. We gotta house and chickens an' fruit trees an' a place a hunderd time prettier than this. An' we got fren's, that's what we got. (p.78)

Curley's wife's threat to have Crooks lynched (hanged) – a brutal execution method used on thousands of African-American people during the nineteenth and twentieth centuries – underlines her inhumanity.

Key point

The novella resists the temptation to present Crooks as an angelic figure without human faults; instead, Steinbeck takes the more complex route of showing the damage done to Crooks' personality by his mistreatment.

Key vocabulary

Booby hatch: a psychiatric institution.

Pitchers: Hollywood movies.

Took a powder: ran away.

Q How sympathetically is Curley's wife represented in this scene?

Section 5 (pp.83–97)

Summary: *The see-sawing between hope and despair reaches its climax in this chapter, as the characters' dreams unravel. After Lennie accidentally kills his pup, he is joined in the barn by Curley's wife. The two talk amicably but after she offers her hair for Lennie to stroke, he holds on too tight and scares her, causing him to unintentionally snap her neck. Lennie flees and the other men find the dead body.*

The ominous opening scene, where Lennie regretfully gazes at a pup he has accidentally killed (p.83), sets the tone for what is to come. Themes that have bubbled beneath the surface of the previous sections – violence, desire, coercion, exploitation – erupt violently in this penultimate section.

Yet even though tragedy laces this section, the fluctuating between hope and violence continues. As she always does, Curley's wife violates the serenity of a man's private space – here, for the last time. Wearing a symbolically tempting red dress, Curley's wife ignores the danger as she talks to Lennie. While on some level her inclusion of Lennie appears to be an act of kindness, it is also highly reckless given Lennie's non-existent impulse control. Even when she is displaying compassion, she does so in a dangerous and illegitimate manner.

At first, the conversation between Lennie and Curley's wife appears to be another affirmation of friendship. Like Aunt Clara, perhaps, Curley's wife has made the decision to take Lennie under her wing. This interpretation, at least, could be supported by her decision to confide in Lennie about her depressing life story (p.87).

Yet the male/female dynamic is so toxic that no such connection is possible. As Steinbeck's definition of friendship is restrictive and male-only, a woman's attempt to form this bond can only represent danger. Even when the story she tells is deserving of sympathy – especially when she confesses, 'I don't *like* Curley. He ain't a nice fella' (p.87) – Curley's wife is shown as blatantly overstepping her boundaries.

In keeping with the novella's negative view of romantic relationships, the climactic scene between Lennie and Curley's wife reads like a vicious parody of a love scene. As Lennie 'moved cautiously close to her, until he was right against her' (p.88), she begins tempting him with talk of feeling 'silk an' velvet' (p.89). Until the end, Curley's wife is oblivious to her fate. Like Lennie himself, she completely lacks the capacity to assess risk.

The details of Lennie's altercation at Weed have set the scene for what is about to happen, making Curley's wife's death predictable for everyone except the victim. Her limited knowledge of Lennie's past makes her actions less reckless than they may at first seem.

Lennie's immediate adoption of childlike language after the killing emphasises his unsuitability for the complex and dangerous world in which he finds himself. The contrast between the violence of his actions and the innocence of his reaction ('I shouldn't of did that. George'll be mad', p.90) demonstrates the consequences of thrusting an individual into a situation they are emotionally unequipped to handle.

Unusually in this dialogue-heavy book, a meditative, languid scene silently observes Curley's wife's body (p.91). As if to make up for the unsympathetic way Steinbeck has presented her story, the depiction of the appalling scene is infused with a sense of sympathy: 'the meanness and the plannings and the discontent and the ache for attention were all gone from her face' (p.91). Yet it is only after her death that Curley's wife is permitted to be a person fully deserving of sympathy.

George's reaction to the killing is revealing – not just for its insights about his own personality, but also for the light it sheds on the sense of hope the novella has sustained right until the end. As George reassures Candy that 'Lennie never done it in meanness' (p.93), he even indulges in a brief fantasy about the possibility of Lennie's escape:

> I guess we gotta get 'im an' lock 'im up. We can't let 'im get away. Why, the poor bastard'd starve.' And he tried to reassure himself. 'Maybe they'll lock 'im up an' be nice to 'im. (p.93)

Of course, the world of *Of Mice and Men* has no place for a person such as Lennie – a reality that George quickly accepts even as Candy is unwilling to let go of the dream of their own ranch. The world's cruel limitations, which George has managed to repress for so long, now come rushing back. Fully admitting to the strength of his delusions, George reflects: 'I should of knew … I guess maybe way back in my head I did' (p.92). As he watches his dreams shatter, George is forced to acknowledge that the dream he and Lennie formed was never realisable.

Key point

Given that the section closes with George's decision to kill Lennie as an act of mercy, the lessons here are complex and ambiguous. Even though the dream that has sustained the men throughout their hardships was unrealistic, it provided hope in a time when optimism was in desperately short supply. Striving for the impossible, Steinbeck suggests, is essential to our humanity.

Q What role does Curley's wife play in her own demise?

Section 6 (pp.98–106)

Summary: *The consequences of Lennie's killing of Curley's wife rapidly unfold. George finds Lennie in the clearing and shoots him in the head before the other men come.*

This abrupt conclusion plays out the inevitabilities established in the previous section. The serenity in the barn following the trauma is suddenly violated when 'a water snake glide[s] smoothly up the pool' (p.98). The violent natural imagery used by Steinbeck in his conclusion serves as a further reminder that the outside world is cold and merciless.

As with many of Lennie's childish actions, his naive conversations with real and imaginary figures from his past highlight his unsuitability for this world. Although he technically kills Curley's wife in the previous section, his sustained detachment from reality leaves no doubt that he is mentally incapable of culpability. Although it is not stated directly, a large part of the blame for Lennie's crime falls on George, who failed to supervise him as he would a young child.

Shortly before George's killing of Lennie, the story of the ranch is recounted one final time (p.102). However, this time there is no masking the unbridgeable gap between the two men. George is recounting a story in which he no longer believes; in contrast, Lennie is incapable of understanding the impossibility of achieving his dream.

How, then, should George's actions towards Lennie be judged? With nothing keeping their dream alive, George's efforts to string Lennie along with a fantasy future can seem cruel and irresponsible. Although the novella's judgement of George is not resolved, the real-life consequences of his Romantic perspective on life become inescapable. George instilled a sense of hope in Lennie – and in himself – that he had no plausible way of realising. While this may have been well-intentioned, it also finally seems like a dangerous denial of life's realities.

Key point

At the novella's conclusion, it is left unclear whether George's commitment to a better life has been helpful or harmful overall.

Q Do you think George's final interaction with Lennie is cruel or kind?

CHARACTERS & RELATIONSHIPS

George

Key quotes

'Guys like us, that work on ranches, are the loneliest guys in the world. They got no family. They don't belong no place ... With us it ain't like that. We got a future.' (to Lennie, p.15)

'Don't let [Curley] pull you in – but – if the son-of-a-bitch socks you – let 'im have it.' (to Lennie, p.31)

'Lennie's so scared all he can think to do is jus' hold on.' (p.42)

'The poor bastard's nuts. Don't shoot 'im. He di'n't know what he was doin'.' (p.96)

George is the most complex character in Steinbeck's novella, mainly because we know more about him than we do about the other characters.

On one level, George is quite like the farm workers who surround him. He is rough and uncultured in his speech, and is shown to have deeply conservative views about women. On the surface, the grumpy and irritable George is rough and emotionally remote, like the others working on the farm. He shares in most of their interests, and consequently has many of their faults.

Yet there is another side to George that sets him apart from his contemporaries. Most importantly, he sacrifices most of his freedom in life by taking on Lennie. It is this compassion that sets George apart from the others in this world. He is secretive and modest, but still cares for Lennie.

George's bitterness about Lennie partly obscures the genuine sacrifices he has made for his friend. Even though George can often be hostile towards Lennie – for example, complaining that he could 'have a girl' (p.9) if he were able to travel alone – his life could have been as aimless as the other men he meets on the ranch if it were not for the burden of caring for Lennie.

George's tough exterior conceals genuine kindness and compassion. His affection and care for Lennie is genuine, but it only emerges under extreme hardship. He strives to protect Lennie in practical ways, including his initial securing of a place to hide in the brush if things go wrong (p.17). Furthermore, his repeated willingness to share the dream of owning his own plot of land with Lennie is George's kindest gesture.

Two examples of George's willingness to protect his friend stand out. The first is the fight with Curley, where George does everything he can to prevent Lennie getting involved before finally urging Lennie to fight back when conflict is inevitable. The second is George's mercy killing of Lennie, which saves him from the brutality that would have been dealt to him by the other farm workers.

Another way the novel points to George's greater virtue is through his affinity with Slim, the idolised farm worker. Slim and George clearly enjoy the beginnings of a friendship, a rare quantity in a world of suspicion, distrust and malice.

Although he is sometimes hostile, George is marked as a good person who clearly deserves a life of peace and fulfilment.

Lennie

Key quotes

'I tried not to forget. Honest to God I did, George.' (p.6)

'Maybe [Lennie] ain't bright, but I never seen such a worker. He damn near killed his partner buckin' barley.' (Slim, pp.39–40)

'George wun't go away and leave me. I know George wun't do that.' (p.73)

'If George sees me talkin' to you he'll give me hell.' (to Curley's wife, p.86)

The 'gentle giant' Lennie has many kind characteristics, most obviously his love for animals. Lennie's efforts to show tenderness to small animals by petting them always end in their accidental deaths. The damage Lennie does to the things he loves reflects the clumsy, uncontrolled way he interacts with the world, a lack of control that ultimately proves catastrophic.

Lennie is utterly dependent on George, making this a highly unequal friendship, akin, in many ways, to a father-son relationship. He 'imitate[s] George exactly' (p.5), and his face becomes 'drawn with terror' (p.13) when George is angry with him. However, the two share a unified dream of owning their own ranch, with the promise of owning his own rabbits sustaining Lennie through hardship.

In a world where suspicion is everywhere, Lennie is an inherently vulnerable character who lacks the basic self-protection mechanisms that others have built up around themselves. As a physically overpowering man, he inevitably draws the ire of other farm workers, who are envious of his natural strength.

While Lennie's fear of violence is in many ways his saving grace, this can't compensate for his failure to regulate his displays of physical affection. This is the major paradox of his character – it is his incessant need to demonstrate his affection that causes harm to others. The series of dead animals scattered throughout the novel, all accidental victims of Lennie's attentions, show how Lennie's impulses are overwhelming in their intensity.

The repetitive nature of Lennie's life plays out like a tragedy. Every time he has an animal, he inadvertently kills it. Every time he meets a woman, he inadvertently terrifies her. These repeated patterns might contain an early clue that Lennie's fantasy of peacefully tending rabbits is doomed. The seed of impulsiveness in his soul will eventually destroy his dreams, as well as those of George.

It is important to Lennie's character that he has nowhere else to go. People who struggle like him were ignored within the society of Steinbeck's time, as they were often confined within institutions and shielded from public view. While it lasts, therefore, his situation as George's companion is a lucky one.

Candy

Key quotes

'I ain't much good with on'y one hand. I lost my hand right here on this ranch. That's why they give me a job swampin'.' (p.59)

'I ought to of shot that dog myself, George. I shouldn't ought to of let no stranger shoot my dog.' (p.61)

'We know what we got, and we don't care whether you know it or not.' (to Curley's wife, p.79)

Candy is the novella's third major point of identification, sketched in with complexity. Candy is marked from the beginning as a kindred spirit with Lennie and George due to his love of his old dog – a mutt with no monetary value (and therefore no reason to exist, according to the other workers). He bonds with Lennie and George over their shared enthusiasm for the dream of settling down, offering to bankroll most of the plan. Sensing that Lennie and George can offer him shelter from a world that has decided he is of little use, Curley latches on to their doomed promise. Like his dog, who is put down at others' urging, Candy is completely at the mercy of others. Having lost full control of his body puts him in an extremely vulnerable position when considered in relation to the brutal existence on farms in the 1930s.

From the time of his dog's death, Candy plays the part of a tragic chorus in *Of Mice and Men* – he observes the action and comments on it, laying bare the exploitative structures of the world in which he is forced to live. By having the most precarious life of all the characters, Candy is a personification of industrial society's underside, as he is seen as little more than human refuse by his indifferent employers.

Yet as soon as Candy has people to anchor himself to, he shows himself capable of great loyalty and kindness. He has an unusual degree of patience for Lennie, perhaps as a result of being similarly disregarded by the able-bodied mainstream. Candy and Lennie are linked by their disadvantages, but only Candy is aware of the nature of his situation. As such, he offers a poignant reminder of life's precarious nature under a system of unregulated capitalism.

Slim

Key quotes

'George looked over at Slim and saw the calm, Godlike eyes fastened on him.' (p.41)

'[Lennie's] jes' like a kid, ain't he.' (p.44)

Slim is perhaps a less compelling character than he first appears. While he is obviously attractive, honest and hardworking, Slim's believability is compromised by his unrealistic level of perfection. He could perhaps be seen as a similar personality to George but with more opportunities in life – the whole farm reveres him as a moral authority, and defers to his judgement when needed. Steinbeck paints him as virtually omniscient: 'His ear heard more than was said to him, and his slow speech had overtones not of thought, but of understanding beyond thought' (p.35).

Slim is the only one to realise that George needs shielding from the world's traumas and injustices; for example, he proposes taking George out for a drink after Lennie's traumatic death. Unlike the men he is surrounded by, Slim is quick to see the good side of people and give them the benefit of the doubt, a virtually unknown concept in this unforgiving world. Steinbeck seems to suggest that, to reform society, we will need a Slim-like reservoir of goodness and tolerance.

The developing friendship between Slim and George could also be seen as the novella's unrealised hope. Whenever they meet, Slim seems to bring out the best in George; Slim could be seen as an idealised version of what George could become if he had more opportunities in life.

Yet Slim's presence may strike a less optimistic note than it appears. Even someone as talented, hardworking and idealised as Slim is trapped in an exploitative relationship with his employer; he 'rules the roost' on the farm, but seems unable to break out on his own. If you are not born into the fortunate class of society, Steinbeck seems to suggest, there's no genuine hope for you to break out of the cycle of poverty and disadvantage that has been ruthlessly implemented by the dominant class. The game is rigged against the 'little guy', no matter how hard they try.

Curley

Key quotes

'Curley's like a lot of little guys. He hates big guys.' (Candy, p.28)

'Seems like Curley is cockier'n ever since he got married.' (Candy, p.29)

'What the hell you laughin' at?' (to Lennie, p.62)

The resentful and aggressive newly married husband of his spontaneous and irrepressible wife, Curley is a character without redeeming features. Slim's opposite, Curley is scarcely a real character. Instead, he is an archetypal villain, fulfilling the opposite function to Slim in terms of his unadulterated embrace of aggressive impulses. In his suggested sexual gluttony, possessiveness and incapability of seeing the good in people, Curley fully vindicates Lennie's prophetic remark that 'this ain't no good place' (p.34). From his lascivious sexual behaviour, which triggers the other men's disgust in his 'glove fulla vaseline' (p.34), to his aggressive jealousy, Curley utterly lacks virtue, courage and human sympathy.

These character flaws make Curley the personification of undeserved, and unfairly exercised, power. His entire way of behaving is made possible by his privileged position on the ranch as the boss' son. His unjust application of vengeance on people who don't deserve it – most notably Lennie, but also his wife – stands in for Steinbeck's disgust at the way systems can oppress the people trapped within them. In the entire novella, we never see Curley carry out a single decent act – yet, Slim aside, he is far more powerful than the other farmhands. This is an implicit criticism of the existing power structure, including how it rewards people worthy of punishment. The way the farm works is the very opposite of a meritocracy. Instead, the best are kept down and the worst rise to the top.

As someone who seems to lack human compassion, Curley's relationships with other people are exploitative. This includes his wife, who is essentially kept under lock and key to guard against his jealousy. His only hobby – boxing – is merely an outlet for his aggression. Despite looming large in the small world of the farm, Curley is friendless; for Steinbeck, with his unfailing emphasis on human companionship, this is the worst fate imaginable.

Crooks

Key quotes

'If I say something, why it's just a nigger sayin' it.' (p.70)

'I tell ya a guy gets too lonely an' he gets sick.' (p.72)

In many ways, Crooks is in a similar position to Candy. As a black man, however, Crooks is even more representative of the inequality of the society against which Steinbeck is railing. While Candy's windfall (cash payment) enables him to have a genuine chance at happiness with George and Lennie, Crooks does not even have this hope granted to him. Everything we know about Crooks suggests a man of integrity and decency, yet he has no real opportunity to interact with the people around him from a position of friendship.

Crooks' possessions symbolise wasted promise: 'he had books, too; a tattered dictionary and a mauled copy of the California civil code for 1905' (p.67). These items show that Crooks' intellectual capacities are stifled by the poverty, racism and isolation he faces. Again and again, we see people forced to squander their innate gifts as they struggle to survive.

Crooks' lack of power is fully exposed when we see him attempt to hold on to the only speck of autonomy he is allowed – by trying to prevent people from visiting his sleeping quarters in the barn, as we see with his hostile reaction to Lennie's intrusion: 'You got no right to come in my room' (pp.66–7). Even this ends in disaster when Curley's wife threatens to have him lynched.

There are some elements of Crooks that seem more like a caricature – someone with impossibly exaggerated characteristics – than a character. For example, his name references his crooked back, which prevents him from participating in the physical life of the farm. This trait, symbolised by the repeated habit of rubbing oil into his back, defines Crooks as the farm scapegoat. He is pain, exclusion and suffering personified.

Unlike Slim, though, Crooks is not an impossibly idealised character. We find that he is capable of cruelty; for example, his face 'light[s] with pleasure in his torture' (p.71) of the vulnerable Lennie, as he sadistically teases him about George being in danger. Yet after Crooks backs off, he soon realises a kindred spirit in Lennie. Crooks is ultimately portrayed as a kind, curious and socially outgoing man, who has only turned inward and become bitter after being subjected to a lifetime of relentless bullying and rejection. All of his positive memories mentioned are from his childhood, before he was old enough to understand that he would never be permitted to belong in a white-dominated society.

Crooks' completely subordinate position makes him a suitable conversationalist for the gregarious (sociable) Slim and the agreeable Lennie. He is a symbol of the deceptive beliefs people form in this brutal world, as he retires 'into the terrible protective dignity of the negro' (p.78) when he becomes scared by Curley's wife's plausible threats. An entirely new dimension of Crooks' character rapidly comes to light as he temporarily begins to believe in the fantasy of escaping to a rural hideaway with George, Lennie and Candy. Of course, this dream is even more implausible for Crooks than it is for the others.

Curley's wife

Key quotes

'I'm glad you bust up Curley a little bit. He got it comin' to him.' (p.81)

'Why can't I talk to you? I never get to talk to nobody. I get awful lonely.' (p.85)

'Well, I wasn't gonna stay no place where I couldn't get nowhere or make something of myself ... So I married Curley.' (p.87)

'You're nuts ... But you're a kinda nice fella. Jus' like a big baby.' (to Lennie, p.89)

Curley's wife is the most mysterious character in *Of Mice and Men*. With her, Steinbeck seems to be working through two opposing impulses – his view of women as temptresses, and his awareness of this trope as demeaning to women. It's hard to know for sure which side Steinbeck comes down on.

Curley's wife is treated with repulsion and loathing by all the men on the ranch – including Curley himself. Even the description of his affection, with his glove 'fulla Vaseline' (p.29), connects her to sexual objectification; for almost all of the novel, she has no independent existence outside other men's opinions of her. It is only shortly before her death that she is finally given the chance to speak.

In many ways, then, Curley's wife has no chance. Apart from Lennie, who views her with unabashed wonder, every other man sees her as sexual temptation in human form. In almost every case, this has nothing to do with her actions. Apart from walking around the farm and mildly flirting with Slim, she does not seem to engage in any of the untoward behaviour of which she is accused. But in a male-centred world that places no value in women's opinions, this counts for nothing.

It is important that George senses the danger posed by Curley's wife immediately. On one level, he is right – she will ultimately spell trouble for Lennie. However, George is wrong in his quickness to condemn Curley's wife herself, rather than the misogynistic world that surrounds her, for the danger she poses. Her actions with Lennie, while naive on her part and ultimately catastrophic, are not calculated. In this final scene, she is only guilty of being *insufficiently* calculating. She is not trying to seduce Lennie, only to treat him with the kindness he seldom receives from others.

Steinbeck, then, subtly shifts the burden of guilt away from Curley's wife. George seems to be using her as a scapegoat to conceal from himself his own responsibility but, ultimately, his failure to supervise Lennie is the main cause of her death. Because George alone fully understands what Lennie is capable of, his visit to the town is clearly a dereliction of his duty of care. This final, tragic event, then, reiterates a major theme of the novel – men unfairly placing the blame on women for their own human failings.

As the novella is so fully invested in the men's perspective, it is far too simplistic to see the character of Curley's wife as a critique of the patriarchal system that overshadows *Of Mice and Men*. Like the Biblical character Lot's wife, who is unfairly held responsible for God's total destruction of the 'sinful' cities of Sodom and Gomorrah, Curley's wife is a modern representation of the woman as a hapless scapegoat. Even though Curley's wife symbolises female temptation and corruption, she is subtly shown to be a better person than she is allowed to be.

THEMES, IDEAS & VALUES

Fate

Key quotes

'I seen too many guys with land in their head. They never get none under their hand.' (Crooks, p.75)

'I think I knowed from the very first. I think I knowed we'd never do her. [Lennie] usta like to hear about it so much I got to thinking maybe we would.' (George, p.93)

The characters in *Of Mice and Men* seem to be bound by a force beyond their control. While the central duo pin their hopes on buying their freedom, this hope seems deluded right from the start.

Steinbeck's world works on the mechanisms of fate, whereby the characters are toyed with by forces beyond their control. Even as they struggle against their situation, they are continually sucked back into the restricted nature of their current lives.

If the force of fate really does play as powerful a part in *Of Mice and Men* as it seems to, the novella is even crueller than it first appears. The men mull over the reality of never really having had a shot at their dream, which seems far more difficult than never having any hope to begin with.

Friendship

Key quotes

'I seen the guys that go around on the ranches alone ... They don't have no fun. After a long time they get mean.' (George, p.41)

'I tell ya a guy gets too lonely an' he gets sick.' (Crooks, p.72)

'We got each other, that's what, that gives a hoot in hell about us.' (George to Lennie, p.103)

One of the novella's most obvious themes is also the most profound. Friendship is the only thing most of the men have to depend on in their lives of poverty and instability. Those without friendship are doomed –

witness the friendless Crooks, a bright soul who wastes away into 'the terrible protective dignity of the negro' (p.78). As Steinbeck recognises, to be socially unconnected is to be spiritually dead.

George and Lennie are, above all, friends – even though theirs is not a friendship of equals. George, as a highly intelligent and savvy man, is obviously cast in the protector role for Lennie, whose lack of emotional maturity and failure to understand the world around him often lead him into trouble. At times, Steinbeck is realistic about the implications of this unequal friendship. Earlier, George admits, he tormented Lennie, despite Lennie not understanding that he was the cause of the danger:

> One day, a bunch of guys was standin' around up the Sacramento River. I was feelin' pretty smart. I turns to Lennie and says, 'Jump in.' An' he jumps. Couldn't swim a stroke. He damn near drowned before we could get him. An' he was so damn nice to me for pullin' him out. Clean forgot I told him to jump in. Well, I ain't done nothing like that no more. (p.41)

Even though Lennie is the butt of this lesson, George does change and improve as he comes to understand the effects of his actions on Lennie. Yet in some ways, the friendship between George and Lennie more resembles that between child and parent, due to Lennie's limited capacities in comparison to George.

Steinbeck features several interesting examples of friendships, the only sparks of light in the novella's grim world. The great, unrealised friendship is the one between Slim and George, which is cut short after the final tragedy. As the two men talk about their pasts, they seem to be on the verge of forming a more equal friendship than George has with Lennie – yet another promise of happiness that can't be realised in Steinbeck's world.

We see the frustrated desire for this blissful state of friendship most vividly in Crooks' interactions with others. Bitterly aware of his unequal status, Crooks lashes out at the farmhands, who fraternise with him without seeing him as an equal in any way. This is most obvious in Crooks' treatment of Lennie, whose stability he toys with by raising scenarios of George being hurt, his face 'lighted with pleasure in his torture' (p.71). Crooks, whose personality has been warped by his isolation, has lost the ability to connect with other people on an equal basis, a tragedy that defines his life.

Masculinity

Key quotes

'[Curley] hates big guys. He's alla time picking scraps with big guys. Kind of like he's mad at 'em because he ain't a big guy.' (Candy, p.28)

'Any you guys seen my wife?' (Curley, p.54)

'You can talk to people, but I can't talk to nobody but Curley. Else he gets mad. How'd you like not to talk to anybody?' (Curley's wife to Lennie, p.85)

The farm, of course, is a male-dominated environment. Masculinity is a concept that has been celebrated endlessly in American (and Australian) culture, most notably in its physically labouring form. The image of the bronzed labouring man, tougher than nails, wielding an axe or riding a horse, is the admiring theme of countless films, novels, plays and paintings.

Yet Steinbeck, while acknowledging the aesthetic attraction of these images, sees masculinity in far more caustic terms. In his view, it seems to be a trap that causes people caught within it to become vile, stunted caricatures of human beings.

The most obvious example of this is Curley. He is so desperate to contain and confine his wife that he lashes out with violent protective impulses wherever possible – most climactically, of course, in his disastrous fight with Lennie (p.63). Curley's apparent hypermasculinity is rooted in cowardice – as a short and slight man, he hides behind his privileged position as the boss' son.

Physical labour

Key quotes

'[Lennie's] a good skinner. He can rassel grain bags, drive a cultivator. He can do anything.' (George, p.24)

'[Lennie] damn near killed his partner buckin' barley.' (Slim, pp.39–40)

Then as now, there was a key understanding in society that nobility could be achieved through physical labour. The work itself done by the people on the farm, while backbreaking, is not seen in itself as exploitative – instead, it is the low rates of pay that Steinbeck singles out as the key injustice.

In a world that dramatically undervalued the labouring class in favour of the professional class, Steinbeck sought to infuse working people with the dignity of physical labour. As Steinbeck said, 'I've always been amused by the contention that brain work is harder than manual labor. I've never known a man to leave a desk for a muck-stick if he could avoid it.' Every element of the men's world is structured around the daily ritual of work, a pursuit that is personified in the idealised persona of Slim, who embodies the noble nature of physical exertion.

The American Dream

Key quotes

'There wouldn't be no more runnin' round the country and gettin' fed by a Jap cook.' (George, p.58)

'Sure, we'd have a little house an' a room to ourself.' (George, p.58)

'We gotta house and chickens an' fruit trees an' a place a hunderd time prettier than this.' (Candy to Curley's wife, p.78)

George and Lennie's shared ambition to own a farm of their own is an example of the elusive American Dream. While this concept is today understood as more of a personal desire for wealth, 'in the 1930s, it meant freedom, mutual respect and equality of opportunity. It had more to do with morality than material success' (Shiller 2017).

This original version of the American Dream has long been associated with Thomas Jefferson's quote from the Declaration of Independence, defending 'life, liberty, and the pursuit of happiness'. The modest nature of the men's dream in *Of Mice and Men* connects it with the term's modest origins; Lennie and George's vision of happiness is merely to exist in freedom, able to pursue their ambitions and improve their lot in life through their own efforts, unhindered by people who wish to exploit them.

Clearly, George and Lennie's modest wish for comfort and independence is a long way away from the version of the American Dream that is being pursued by the people in charge. Steinbeck implies that American society has detached itself from the original meaning of the American Dream in order to pursue wealth for its own sake, no matter who is hurt in the process. For Steinbeck, the only way to rescue these lost ideals is to properly look after the people who are being neglected, abused and forgotten.

Paradise

Key quotes

'Must be nice to have a room all to yourself this way.' (Lennie to Crooks, p.74)

'An' they'd of been a pig and chickens ... an' in the winter ... the little fat stove ... an' the rain comin' ... an' us jus' settin' there.' (Candy, p.94)

Is paradise a real place or is it a symptom of human delusion? *Of Mice and Men* veers uncomfortably between these two extremes.

Throughout most of the story, the presence of paradise is palpable and believable. The farm imagined by George and Lennie, which is subsequently adopted as a dream by Candy and Crooks, is clearly drawn from Christian ideas of paradise as the promised land. Unlike disembodied visions of heaven, though, theirs is a tangible, pulsing and earthy version of the myth.

Famously, most of the Bible doesn't mention heaven in much detail at all. Writers who have commented on the Bible, though, have tried to imagine what Christ's vision of paradise would be like. This can be seen in the little-read conclusion of Dante's *Divine Comedy*, when the pilgrims enter paradise:

> O grace abounding and allowing me to dare
> to fix my gaze on the Eternal Light,
> so deep my vision was consumed in it!

This rarefied, disembodied vision of paradise in the Christian tradition collides with Steinbeck's view of paradise as something that is firmly bound up with the physical processes of the earth:

> When the fruit come in we could can it – and tomatoes, they're easy to can. Ever' Sunday we'd kill a chicken or a rabbit. Maybe we'd have a cow or a goat, and the cream is so God damn thick you got to cut it with a knife and take it out with a spoon. (p.57)

George's vision, then, involves a return to a simpler, more earthly vision of paradise, as opposed to the more complex and unrelatable theories of Christian doctrine. Steinbeck grimly jokes that the two men's shared vision of paradise is no more attainable for them in this life than heaven would be in the next one.

Social Darwinism

Key quote

'She slang her pups last night ... Nine of 'em. I drowned four of 'em right off. She couldn't feed that many.' (Slim, p.36)

The novella's moral outlook would not be explicable without reference to the considerable influence of Darwinism on American culture. Darwin's *Origin of Species* replaced the idea of a stately, ordered and divinely ordained nature with one that, in the poet Tennyson's words, was 'red in tooth and claw'. In America, this brutal, winner-takes-all idea of nature was adopted by capitalist industrialists as social Darwinism –

the idea that the injustices and inequalities in society were simply how the world worked, and nothing could be done about them.

While social Darwinism has been discredited, in part due to its role in inspiring fascism, its spectre is still with us. Steinbeck held an ambivalent attitude towards this way of thinking, which was highly influential during the writing of *Of Mice and Men*. While he believed that there were serious injustices in society, he strongly disagreed with the hard-line social Darwinists' argument that this situation was somehow 'natural'. Instead, Steinbeck implied, the inequalities in American society could be softened with better treatment from employers, coupled with intelligent government intervention.

Socialism

Key quotes

'The boss was expectin' you last night ... He was sore as hell when you wasn't here to go out this morning.' (Candy, to George and Lennie, p.20)

'When they can me here I wisht somebody'd shoot me. But they won't do nothing like that. I won't have no place to go, an' I can't get no more jobs.' (Candy, p.60)

Steinbeck believed strongly in at least some aspects of socialism (i.e. the use of government power to alleviate poverty). By showing the misery created when people are left entirely by themselves, Steinbeck aimed to show how the US' capitalist system was failing people.

The economic meltdown caused by the Wall Street Crash of 1929 plunged millions of Americans into poverty. Steinbeck's writings roughly coincide with the ascent of Franklin Theodore Roosevelt (FDR) to the presidency in 1932, taking over from Herbert Hoover, whose economic policies were widely seen as disastrous. To his critics, FDR was seen as a socialist for his expansion of the role of government in people's lives.

FDR's New Deal aimed to overhaul the US economy by radically increasing direct government intervention in financial affairs. After his election victory, he adopted many socialist policies, including the minimum wage, back-to-work schemes and social security. While World War II was the event that dragged the US economy out of the Great Depression and paved the way for decades of prosperity, FDR's election was the beginning of the adoption of a range of socialist policies in the US.

Of Mice and Men takes place during the depths of the Great Depression, when FDR's economic New Deal measures had not yet been introduced. Instead, people were left to struggle alone, barely surviving on their farmers' wages. By laying bare the inadequacy of government support systems for the poor, Steinbeck is implying that a more equal way of dividing the wealth of society is required to provide a fairer standard of living for all. As someone who is no longer seen as useful to the economic system, Candy exemplifies this sense of injustice: 'I got hurt four years ago ... They'll can me purty soon. Jus' as soon as I can't swamp out no bunk houses they'll put me on the county' (p.60).

Importantly, the ideology of socialism was viewed very differently in 1937, *Of Mice and Men*'s year of publication, from the way it is viewed today. The Russian Revolution had stunned the world two decades earlier, and capitalist nations were reeling from a series of shocks that led many to think that a socialist takeover of America was plausible. Because communism, as defined by Karl Marx, is inherently an international movement, many people expected that other countries would follow Russia's lead and become communist. Due to its advanced economy, the US was seen as a prime target for a communist takeover.

Steinbeck's hostility to the industrial forces that exploited farm workers across the US has been well documented. We chiefly see life from the side of labouring men in his books; *Of Mice and Men*'s sole representative of industrial power is the exploitative Curley, serenely protected from consequences by his relationship to the boss. In Steinbeck's view, common people's lives can never be improved by those above them in the social ladder because they have too many vested interests.

Sexism

Key quotes

'Don't you even take a look at that bitch.' (George to Lennie, p.33)

'You wasn't no good. You ain't no good now, you lousy tart.' (Candy to Curley's wife, p.94)

While the book is in many ways progressive for its time, its attitude towards women is ambivalent. On one hand, Steinbeck takes pains to show us the imprisoning effects of farm life on a woman, Curley's wife. Although we don't even know her name, Steinbeck is careful to provide us with her dismal backstory; she is a woman who can't escape the orbit of powerful, exploitative men.

The farm workers' views support these ultra-conservative ideas of woman as entities that can pull men down and destroy them. As George warns Lennie:

> 'Listen to me, you crazy bastard,' he said fiercely. 'Don't you even take a look at that bitch. I don't care what she says and what she does. I seen 'em poison before, but I never seen no piece of jail bait worse than her. You leave her be.' (p.33)

Yet Steinbeck's stance is more ambiguous than this reading would suggest. There is a far more sinister reading of the woman in the novella – that of a repository of sin. It is a testament to the influence of misogyny on our lives that even someone as progressive as Steinbeck can use the woman in the tale as 'bait' for the hapless Lennie.

The lure of Curley's wife is connected to her role as a woman; her sexual allure is depicted as a destabilising force that brings down the fragile idyll created within the farm. The lure of women is actually seen elsewhere in the novella too, with George's visit to a brothel the catalyst for Lennie being left alone. In both cases, women – even if they don't mean it – are responsible for men's downfall.

Racism

Key quotes

'Listen, Nigger ... You know what I can do to you if you open your trap?' (Curley's wife to Crooks, p.80)

'A coloured man got to have some rights even if he don't like 'em.' (Crooks, p.81)

The character of Crooks exemplifies the mistreatment of people of colour in the US at this time. Crooks is an oppressed member of the farm, confined to the barn and forbidden to fraternise with the labourers. His acute loneliness is dramatised by his action of repeatedly rubbing his own back with oil to salve his pain, a metaphor for his isolation.

During this time, the US was governed by so-called Jim Crow laws, which legalised racial segregation, forcing white and black people into separate areas of life. For example, black people were unable to travel in certain sections of public transport – a law that Rosa Parks famously protested against in 1955, leading to her arrest. Crooks' situation vividly illustrates the nature of racial conflict burning across the US at that time.

When creating characters, Steinbeck often overcompensated for society's racism by showing his minority characters as morally superior to the white characters around them. For example, although Crooks' intellectual instincts are thwarted by his poverty and isolation, his study of books paints him as intellectually superior to his contemporaries.

The fragility of Crooks' situation is shown by the callous, racist threats of Curley's wife (which severely threatens her position as a sympathetic character):

> She turned on him in scorn. 'Listen, Nigger,' she said. 'You know what I can do to you if you open your trap?' Crooks stared helplessly at her, and then he sat down on his bunk and drew into himself. (p.80)

The ability of Crooks to 'reduc[e] himself to nothing' (p.80) when threatened by a white person is a perfect illustration of the invisibility that black people had to assume when confronted by white people's authority. As Crooks knows, resisting this reality could mean death.

The treatment of disabled people

Key quotes

'George's hand remained outstretched imperiously. Slowly, like a terrier who doesn't want to bring a ball to its master, Lennie approached, drew back, approached again.' (p.10)

'Why [Lennie would] do any damn thing I tol' him. If I tol' him to walk over a cliff, over he'd go.' (George to Slim, p.41)

Steinbeck has received some criticism for his depiction of Lennie, with some calling the representation insulting to people with disabilities. However, this issue is quite complex. Should Steinbeck be praised for depicting a character with an intellectual disability as a real person, at a time when this was extremely rare in fiction, or does he deserve condemnation for portraying Lennie as 'subhuman'?

In at least one way, Steinbeck is compassionate towards Lennie. He goes to great lengths to show how the novella's 'good' characters – mainly George, Candy and Slim – interpret Lennie's personality; for example, Slim 'can see [that] Lennie ain't a bit mean' (p.42).

As Slim's judgement is described as 'godlike', his assessment of Lennie is to be trusted. Lennie clearly never displays malice towards another person, unlike many of the workers surrounding him. He is a pacifist (someone who rejects violence) as well as an animal lover, two more traits with positive associations (even though these are obviously distorted when filtered through Lennie's unregulated behaviour). Despite the grief and tragedy Lennie causes at multiple points, his decency is never in doubt.

Critics of Steinbeck, though, have raised a more difficult criticism with the author's portrayal:

> Lennie is further identified as un-human through the many descriptions of him as animal. He is described, variously, as having paws, as growling, as moving as a bear moves, as drinking like a horse, as being as strong as a bull, as being like a terrier with a ball. Each of these dehumanise him. (Lawrence 2020)

Steinbeck does indeed depict Lennie in these animalistic terms. Thus, we are faced with the difficult situation of acknowledging that Steinbeck's view of Lennie is insulting to people with disabilities in some ways, yet compassionate in others.

Animism

Key quotes

'As happens sometimes, a moment settled and hovered and remained for much more than a moment. And sound stopped and movement stopped for much, much more than a moment.' (p.91)

'Already the sun had left the valley to go climbing up the slopes of the Gabilan mountains, and the hilltops were rosy in the sun.' (p.98)

Steinbeck saw himself as a naturalistic writer, dedicated to representing the 'truth' of human experience. This set him against the more mannered writing of many of his contemporaries, who were more interested in the activities of high society than the working class, which was not often seen as a legitimate subject for 'serious' fiction.

Yet at certain moments in *Of Mice and Men*, Steinbeck's commitment to the themes of his writing brings him to go against the grain of the documentary writing style for which he was aiming. The most obvious example is Steinbeck's use of the physical environment as something that is alive, with its own agency. The settings in which his characters live often seems to comment on what is happening in the novella, or prepare us, the reader, for what is about to happen.

There are many instances in the novella of animal spirits seemingly commenting on the fate of the men. This suggests that Steinbeck didn't see nature as a neutral backdrop to his realistic action, but rather as an active force. The most obvious example of this animated description of nature is the scene that unfolds shortly before Lennie's death:

> A water snake glided smoothly up the pool … A silent head and beak lanced down and plucked it out by the head, and the beak swallowed the little snake while its tail waved frantically. (p.98)

This depiction of the pitiless conflict between animals is placed very tellingly in the book, coming right before the inevitable final tragedy. The helpless snake here could be interpreted as Lennie, and the 'silent head and beak' could be interpreted as the forces of fate that send him to his doom.

This use of nature to add a layer of description to the action between human characters is obviously a non-realistic technique. Steinbeck's use of the natural world as a participant in the action has a lot in common with the idea of animism:

> The person or social group with an 'animistic' sensibility attributes sentience – or the quality of being 'animated' – to a wide range of beings in the world, such as the environment, other persons, animals, plants, spirits, and forces of nature like the ocean, winds, sun, or moon. (Swancutt 2019)

The characters in *Of Mice and Men* are not just surrounded by physical matter; they seem to inhabit a natural world that is somehow aware of and responsive to their presence. By using nature as a way to reflect on the fates of his characters, Steinbeck displays a more 'mystical' way of looking at the world than his more traditional working-class themes might suggest.

Violence and pacifism

Key quotes

'I don't care if you're the best welter in the country. You come for me, an' I'll kick your God damn head off.' (Carlson to Curley, p.62)

'But Lennie watched in terror the flopping little man whom he held.' (p.63)

The half-savage vision of nature in *Of Mice and Men* is reflected in the human world. At the Salinas farmhouse, violence often seems to be the only realistic means of solving problems. Many of the stories George and Lennie hear from the other men involve violence, or the threat of future violence.

This all-pervasive readiness to resort to violence as a problem-solving mechanism is shown to have serious consequences on the men's characters – even the most sympathetic ones. For instance, when Candy discusses the fight between Crooks and a former employee, Smitty, there is a disturbing gap between the brutality of what he is describing and the sheer enjoyment with which he describes it, pausing between the retelling 'in relish of the memory':

> Jesus, we had fun. They let the nigger come in that night. Little skinner name of Smitty took after the nigger. Done pretty good, too. The guys wouldn't let him use his feet, so the nigger got him. If he coulda used his feet, Smitty says he woulda killed the nigger. (p.22)

This story, told excitedly by Candy – who is one of the novel's more sympathetic characters – clearly shows how violence has lost its meaning, becoming merely a trivial form of entertainment that dehumanises both participants and spectators. Candy's racially derogatory references to Crooks, as well as his perverse view of the fight as a source of satisfaction and amusement, show the moral corruption that the farm environment has inflicted on these men's minds. As their bloodthirsty, brutal dismissal of Crooks demonstrates, these are deeply damaged people.

Ironically, the novella's only completely pacifist character, Lennie, is the one who unintentionally commits violent acts that only lead to a further spiral of violence. Even when he is justified in committing violence, as he is against Curley during their fight, the consequences of his choice are disastrous. In a morally hopeless world such as Steinbeck's Salinas of the early 1930s, there does not seem to be any avenue for pacifism to be a viable option.

DIFFERENT INTERPRETATIONS

Different interpretations arise from different responses to a text. Over time, a text will evoke a wide range of responses from its readers, who may come from various social or cultural groups and live in very different places and historical periods. Responses by critics and reviewers can be published in newspapers, journals and books, both online and in print. They can also be expressed in discussions among readers in the media, classrooms, book groups and so on.

While there is no single correct reading or interpretation of a text, it is important to understand that an interpretation is more than a personal opinion – it is the justification of a point of view on the text. To present an interpretation of a text based on your point of view, you must use a logical argument and support it with relevant evidence from the text.

Critical viewpoints

Of Mice and Men was highly anticipated by the public and positively received by most critics on its publication. The simplicity and directness of the story was highly praised, as was the naturalistic language.

Yet a strong counter-narrative to this backdrop of praise was started by the famous and influential American critic Edmund Wilson, who criticised Steinbeck's novel for its efforts to 'present life in animal terms'. By showing his characters as trapped like animals within a dark fate, Steinbeck was seen by Wilson as overly deterministic – in other words, he denied the importance of people's agency to improve their circumstances.

Since then, *Of Mice and Men* has been frequently criticised for its use of derogatory language towards women and people of colour. For this reason, it has been frequently included on banned books lists in various school libraries. Despite the fact that Steinbeck included these terms to criticise his characters' viewpoints, the pressure to ban the book has never diminished.

Two interpretations of *Of Mice and Men*

Interpretation 1: *Of Mice and Men* is an optimistic book about the triumph of the human spirit.

From the beginning, George and Lennie are thrown into a bleak, grim and impoverished world in which nobody is looking out for them. Ostracised and desperate, their options are virtually limited to survival. At the novella's commencement, their situation seems utterly hopeless.

Yet as the grinding, impoverished lives of George and Lennie unfold over the next few days, something unexpected happens. A genuine sense of hope for the two men arises, and remains undiminished by the appalling conditions they are forced into.

This enduring sense of hope is expressed in the pair's shared fantasy of having their own piece of land. As readers, our knowledge of the book's ending distorts how we see the pair's repeated, joyous descriptions of this dream. Yet even though the friends fail to achieve their dream, this failure hardly matters. It's the journey, not the destination that counts, as the two men's shared commitment to making their future happen propels them through their difficult lives.

The value of having a dream is obvious, as George and Lennie are surrounded by people who have given up on life: Crooks, whose isolation has turned him against his fellow man; Curley, whose jealousy has dehumanised him and turned him into a sadist and coward; the boss, who seems to care little for the welfare of his workers; Whit and Carlson, whose cynicism has made them incapable of genuine friendship and sincere feeling for others; and Curley's wife, whose loneliness can only be expressed in sexual terms. The all-encompassing rot makes Lennie and George's central friendship burn more brightly.

The pair's ambition to make the most out of their unpromising lives is made more appealing by George's realistic perspective about what they can achieve. As the more capable member of the pair, George never deludes himself that spending his life with Lennie is an optimal outcome. Instead, he spitefully acknowledges that their current situation is undesirable: 'I could get along so easy and so nice if I didn't have you on my tail. I could live so easy and maybe have a girl' (p.9).

Yet despite all his grumbling, George does not in fact leave Lennie until he is absolutely forced to. The strength of his dedication is admirable because George seems genuinely committed to a shared life with his friend. Lennie regularly tests George's patience, but these setbacks matter less than his belief in the value of their shared friendship, which seems to protect George against becoming depressed by an unforgiving world. Even though George ultimately loses Lennie, he has gained from the experience. George has grown as a person for participating in their imagined future together.

Lennie's view of the friendship is less complex. He obviously gains immeasurably from George's presence. By entering the fantasy future George creates, Lennie gains a slender thread of hope that propels him through life. As the men form plans for their future, Lennie's participation in the telling of the tale provides him with his sole source of happiness.

Even though the story of the farm is told multiple times by Lennie and George, the novella never takes an unrealistic view of the difficulties they are facing; at no point does Steinbeck suggest that escape from their predicament will be easy. Yet the affection that the dream inspires in each man's heart ultimately makes *Of Mice and Men* a hopeful story of mutual affection.

When everything comes crashing down around the two men, it is tempting to see this conclusion as a blow against the characters' hubris (arrogance). In other words, Steinbeck could have been making the point that dreaming of a better life was not something they, as labourers, were entitled to do. But *Of Mice and Men* sees the friends' shared dream far more positively. It is George and Lennie's willingness to dream against the odds that separates them from most of the other men, whose only source of escape from their drudgery is visiting the local brothel.

Lennie and George's willingness to imagine something better has parallels with a religious experience. The pair's unshakeable faith that they will reach the promised land echoes the leap of faith that is required for wholehearted belief in a higher power – even in the face of desperation.

While it is true that Lennie and George's dream fails to eventuate, their ability to believe in something better than their current reality elevates them to a higher plane. Their dream may be deluded and unrealistic, but it is also seen as noble; sustaining hope requires a refusal to lie down and take whatever the world dishes out to them.

In a sense, Lennie and George's failure to achieve their dream actually makes it *more* profound, not less. Amid the squalor of the bunkhouse and the hostility and violence of others, Lennie and George's dream provides a meditative, sacred space that they both inhabit. The dream is never explained away by Lennie's naivety; every time George tells the story, he is equally affected by it. As he dramatises the story to Lennie, for example, Steinbeck observes that 'his voice was growing warmer' (p.57). Their shared vision of heaven on earth brings out each man's best self.

Interpretation 2: *Of Mice and Men* is a pessimistic book that depicts every character as trapped in a nightmare from which there is no escape.

There are few places bleaker than the farmstead in which Lennie and George find themselves during *Of Mice and Men*. Pictured as an unholy hell on earth from the beginning, the farmhouse resembles a prison that consumes everyone unfortunate enough to enter it.

In Steinbeck's novella, every hope that life offers is ripped away from the men before they have had even a small chance to sample it. All the hopes and dreams in the world – including romantic relationships, stable employment and spiritual satisfaction – are dangled before Lennie and George before being cruelly taken away.

The promise of happiness in the novella, then, is merely a prelude to George's eventual misery. Steinbeck's moral lesson is clear: in a universe of limited promise, dreaming big is a guaranteed path to self-destruction. To illustrate this point, the only happy character in the book is the one that refuses to have dreams beyond his current life. This is Slim, a 'jerkline skinner, the prince of the ranch' (p.34).

Slim is a man of great potential – and more importantly, he has *fully reached* this potential as a farm labourer. He is happy with his limited station, and works to make the most of it. It is Slim, not George or Lennie, who offers the book's only moments of lightness and hope. Consider how limited Slim's situation is, and how much he makes of it. His entire identity is subsumed into his work, in which he takes great pride. Beyond his fairness in relation to other men, we learn nothing about his aspirations beyond the ranch. It is only by forbidding himself to harbour unrealistic fantasies of creating a heaven on earth that his character becomes the only one capable of achieving contentment.

In contrast, Steinbeck repeatedly shows us the damage done by placing unrealistic expectations on one's own life. Each man who dares to dream in *Of Mice and Men* is consumed in the process. After hearing about Lennie and George's dream of escape, Crooks tries to bring Lennie's expectations down to earth by explaining this unbearable reality: 'Ever'body wants a little piece of lan'. I read plenty of books out here. Nobody never gets to heaven, and nobody gets no land. It's just in their head' (p.73).

Crooks speaks the truth. He knows the danger of believing that this world will ever furnish anything more than the bare necessities. This is why he is so embittered about the loss of his own childhood, which has clear parallels with George and Lennie's fantasy:

> My old man had a chicken ranch, 'bout ten acres. The white kids come to play at our place, an' sometimes I went to play with them, and some of them was pretty nice. My ol' man didn't like that. I never knew till long later why he didn't like that. But I know now. (p.70)

Crooks' life unfolds as a series of crushing disappointments. Over the course of his life, he has been broken down from a happy, friendly child from a land-owning family to a bitter, solitary and often-sadistic figure confined to a dank barn. He, of all people, understands the damage that can be done to someone's personality by latching onto dreams that can't be accommodated by an unyielding reality.

The America of the early 1930s in Steinbeck's novella is nothing more than an unfeeling machine that strips wealth from the deserving and throws all those with dreams on the ash heap. All those characters who seem cynical, negative or hostile are simply taking sensible measures to protect themselves from further disappointment.

This may seem like a winning strategy – and compared to the despair that Lennie, George, Candy and finally Crooks inflict on themselves, it probably is. But staying realistic in such an unpromising world takes a terrible toll on people's souls. All around Lennie and George are people who have flattened out their human qualities until they are simply workers, good for little except herding cattle and pitching horseshoes in an endlessly repetitive game of downtrodden life.

The only solution to this often-repeated situation, Steinbeck seems to imply, is one that lies outside the confines of the farmhouse: massive structural reform, achievable only through imposing massive political change from the top down. Yet politics is barely mentioned in the novella, suggesting that the farm workers completely lack any understanding of the forces keeping them down. The exploitative relationship between landowner and worker is seen by most of the characters simply as the way things are.

Even though Steinbeck was an ardent advocate for reforming labour laws to prevent situations like those in *Of Mice and Men*, the only alternative vision that the novella is able to conjure is a fantasy-based one. As George eventually admits, 'I should of knew … I guess maybe way back in my head I did' (p.92). The drive to escape to a space that only exists in four people's minds suggests a complete failure to imagine a realistic alternative to their current lives. Even after George has pledged to save everything he earns, his and Lennie's eventual escape would have been impossible without Candy's unexpected financial contribution. The system is so broken for regular people that improvement is unimaginable outside fantasy.

In their persistent passion, George and Lennie present bright spots against the dark background of their surroundings. Most of their behaviour and dedication is admirable, or at least understandable. Yet the glimpses of goodness we see through their care for each other, and also through the brief window of hope offered to Candy, simply makes the final disappointment seem more crushing when it arrives.

Every day spent on the farmstead brings the characters in *Of Mice and Men* further away from the qualities of kindness and fraternity that would be required to create meaningful social change. Instead, the economic system represented by the farmhouse, and the virtually unceasing exploitation it enables, confines characters to their immediate present without any hope of a reprieve.

QUESTIONS & ANSWERS

This section focuses on your own analytical writing on the text, and gives you strategies for producing high-quality responses in your coursework and exam essays.

Essay writing – an overview

An essay on a literary work is a formal and serious piece of writing that presents your point of view on the text, usually in response to a given topic. Your 'point of view' in an essay is your interpretation of the meaning of the text's language, structure, characters, situations and events, supported by detailed analysis of textual evidence.

Analyse – don't summarise

In your essays it is important to avoid simply summarising what happens in a text.

- A **summary** is a description or paraphrase (retelling in different words) of the characters and events. For example: 'Macbeth has a horrifying vision of a dagger dripping with blood before he goes to murder King Duncan.'
- An **analysis** is an explanation of the real meaning or significance that lies 'beneath' the text's words (and images, for a film). For example: 'Macbeth's vision of a bloody dagger shows how deeply uneasy he is about the violent act he is contemplating, and conveys his sense that supernatural forces are impelling him to act.'

A limited amount of summary is sometimes necessary to let your reader know which part of the text you wish to discuss. However, always keep this to a minimum and follow it immediately with your analysis of what this part of the text is really telling us.

Plan your essay

Carefully plan your essay so that you have a clear idea of what you are going to say. The plan ensures that your ideas flow logically, that your argument remains consistent and that you stay on the topic. An essay plan should be a list of **brief dot points** covering no more than half a page.

- Include your central argument or main contention – a concise statement of your overall response to the topic.
- Write three or four dot points for each paragraph, indicating the main idea and evidence/examples from the text. Note that in your essay you will need to *expand* on these points and *analyse* the evidence.

Structure your essay

An essay is a complete, self-contained piece of writing. It has a clear beginning (the introduction), middle (several body paragraphs) and end (the last paragraph or conclusion). It must also have a central argument that runs throughout, linking each paragraph to form a coherent whole. See examples of introductions and conclusions in the 'Analysing a sample topic' and 'Sample answer' sections.

The introduction establishes your overall response to the topic. It includes your main contention and outlines the main evidence you will refer to in the course of the essay. Write your introduction *after* you have done a plan and *before* you write the rest of the essay.

The body paragraphs argue your case – they present evidence from the text and explain how this evidence supports your argument. Each body paragraph needs:

- a strong **topic sentence** (usually the first sentence) that states the main point being made in the paragraph
- **evidence** from the text, including some brief quotations
- **analysis** of the textual evidence, with **explanation** of its significance and how it supports your argument
- **links back to the topic** in one or more statements, usually towards the end of the paragraph.

Connect the body paragraphs so that your discussion flows smoothly. Use some linking words and phrases such as 'similarly' and 'on the other hand', though don't start every paragraph like this. Another strategy is to use a significant word from the last sentence of one paragraph in the first sentence of the next.

Use key terms from the topic – or synonyms for them – throughout, so the relevance of your discussion to the topic is always clear.

The conclusion ties everything together and finishes the essay. It includes strong statements that emphasise your central argument and provide a clear response to the topic.

Avoid simply restating the points made earlier in the essay – this will end on a very flat note and imply that you have run out of ideas and vocabulary. The conclusion should be a logical extension of what you have written, not just a repetition or summary of it. Writing an effective conclusion can be a challenge. Try using these tips:

- Start by linking back to the final sentence of the second-last paragraph, rather than leaping to your main contention straight away – this helps your writing to flow.
- Use synonyms and expressions with equivalent meanings to vary your vocabulary. This allows you to reinforce your line of argument without being repetitive.
- When planning your essay, think of one or two broad statements or observations about the text's wider meaning. These should be related to the topic and your overall argument. Keep them for the conclusion, since they will give you something 'new' to say but still follow logically from your discussion. The introduction will be focused on the topic, but the conclusion can present a wider view of the text.

Essay topics

1. '*Of Mice and Men* is an ode to the power of friendship.' Discuss.
2. What does *Of Mice and Men* reveal about the effects of poverty on people's behaviour?
3. 'Although Lennie in *Of Mice and Men* is portrayed as a person with a good heart, Steinbeck's characterisation of him is ultimately dehumanising towards people with disabilities.' Do you agree?
4. 'The 'paradise' imagined by George and Lennie in *Of Mice and Men* is nothing more than a harmful delusion.' Discuss.
5. 'The central characters in *Of Mice and Men* are destroyed by their dreams.' Discuss.
6. How does Steinbeck build up an atmosphere of dread in *Of Mice and Men*?
7. 'In Steinbeck's *Of Mice and Men*, female characters struggle as much as their male counterparts.' To what extent do you agree?
8. 'Despite his relatively minor role, Crooks faces the bleakest situation in *Of Mice and Men*.' Do you agree?
9. "I seen the guys that go around on the ranches alone … After a long time they get mean. They get wantin' to fight all the time."
   'An addiction to violence as a way to solve problems is the novella's major source of evil.' Discuss.
10. 'Despite the tragic end to their quest, George and Lennie never become corrupted by their surroundings.' To what extent do you agree?

Analysing a sample topic

This section leads you through the analysis of a sample topic and the planning of a response.

'Although Steinbeck is quick to identify social problems in *Of Mice and Men*, he offers no viable solutions.' Do you agree?

As this topic is focused on social problems, you must first identify which of these (and how many) you will address in your response. While there are a myriad of social problems explored in the text (e.g. poverty, exploitation of workers, sexism, racism, treatment of disabled people), you should try to limit your response to two or three, so that you can discuss each in depth.

Your argument in response to this topic can either be in full agreement (e.g. Steinbeck either does or does not offer viable solutions) or it can be a more nuanced approach where you argue that solutions are provided to some social problems but not all.

One possible response to this topic is explored in the following essay outline.

Sample introduction

> The farm in *Of Mice and Men* is indeed a microcosm of the desperate problems ravaging America during the 1930s. Even those who are fully employed in this system perch precariously above the poverty line. After reading the novella, the reader is more clearly aware of the injustices perpetuated by the farm system on the hapless employees. However, as the work is primarily a description of what has gone wrong, solutions to these nightmarish problems are nowhere to be found.

Body paragraph outline

Paragraph 1: The toll of physical labour

- The reality of farm life for the workers is exhausting. Furthermore, there is a massive power imbalance between workers and employers, and a complete lack of workplace protections.
- The exhaustion of the workers is shown by the subdued mood in the bunkhouse.
- Life outside work is virtually non-existent for the people working on the farm. There is little else to do, with amusement limited to horseshoe throwing and fighting.
- There appear to be no opportunities for the men to find partners, with their interactions with women confined to brothels.

Paragraph 2: The precariousness of life

- The example of Candy shows how expendable people are on the farm.
- Candy's role as a worker is no longer useful, so he must be 'put out to pasture' like his dog. He is fortunate to have savings, but there is no mercy shown to him by his employer.
- The fragility of Candy's life makes his turning to George and Lennie's plan as salvation understandable. Without this dream, he would have no future, yet even this falls through, leaving him in the same situation as at the start of novella.

Paragraph 3: The men's reliance on violence to solve problems

- There is a huge appetite for violence among the workers, which is seen as the sole means of settling disputes.
- This is a consequence of people not having the power to solve their problems legitimately through legal avenues.
- The over-eagerness to fight makes the men chronically mistrustful and hostile towards one another.

Sample conclusion

By the time of Lennie's tragic death, the reader has witnessed cruelty and suffering on multiple levels. Most of the men who work the fields of the absent boss are perpetually ground down, unable to escape the punishing toll of daily hard labour or to amass enough funds to escape the cycle. Lennie's initial judgement that 'this ain't no good place' is amply proven, as the men dutifully engage in the daily labour that only perpetuates the cycle of poverty. While it is true that Lennie and George have hope for their future, this is dependent on the variable of Candy's lifetime savings. Without it, they would never be able to earn the capital to get out of their situation, despite being extremely hard workers. This strongly suggests that Steinbeck does not put forward any viable solutions to the men's plight.

SAMPLE ANSWER

'Despite his relatively minor role, Crooks faces the bleakest situation in *Of Mice and Men*.' Do you agree?

On the surface, Crooks' character is yet another story of mistreatment in a sea of suffering around him. As there are many people barely staying afloat in *Of Mice and Men*, it may not be easy to single his treatment out as a special case. And yet his position is made worse than those around him for several reasons: firstly, Crooks' inability to mix with other men makes his life far more painful than those of the others living on the farm, who can at least take simple pleasure from one another's company; secondly, the social exclusion he has experienced throughout his life has scarred him mentally, limiting his ability to open up to others; and lastly, his intellect and unfulfilled promise makes his repressed existence even bleaker.

The physical scene of Crooks' isolation is the beginning of his misery. His thirst for other people's company gained an outlet at an early age, when 'the white kids come to play at our place, an' sometimes I went to play with them, and some of them was pretty nice'. Yet this promising beginning reaches a grim conclusion in his later life: 'now there ain't a colored man on this ranch an' there's jus' one family in Soledad'. While at least the other men's lives represent an attempt to reach out to others in order to make their time more bearable, Crooks' trajectory is increasingly dark. Confined to the stable for the entirety of the novella, he is placed in an animal-like position from the beginning. The scars this ostracism leaves on Crooks' dignity are highly visible; they are a spiritual equivalent to his excruciating back ailment, which condemns him to a life of physical pain. Every example of Crooks' interaction with other people is mercenary or degraded. The closest he comes to normality is being allowed to play horseshoes with the farm workers, in a short-lived ritual of inclusion; however, this ends in violence at least once. As the game ends, the other men are able to go back to their bunkhouse to fraternise; meanwhile, Crooks is sent back to what is essentially a lifetime of solitary confinement. This terrible separation from his fellow human beings has corrosive effects on Crook's personality. While he is a well-educated and knowledgeable man who would presumably enjoy conversing about important issues and ideas with other people, the only real opportunity he has to talk with them is to enforce the only asset he has in the world: his privacy. This is the reason he so jealously guards his privacy in the barn, which the other men treat with such casual disrespect.

As someone who has been excluded his whole life, Crooks still bears the scars of the miserable treatment he has received. This is made evident when Lennie enters the barn in which Crooks resides: 'I seen your light. I thought I could jus' come in an' set'. Despite Lennie's innocent reasons for being in the barn, Crooks begins turning the malice that others have habitually shown to him onto the innocent Lennie. To rouse Lennie into a state of anguish, for example, Crooks implies that George may be liable to abandon him: 's'pose George don't come back no more'. Lennie gradually wins Crooks over with his 'disarming smile', until Crooks understands that Lennie sees him as a human being like himself. For the first time, Crooks is faced with the prospect of speaking to someone on an equal footing. This brief moment of connection merely heightens the anguish when it is taken away from him, which occurs when Curley's wife enters the barn and casually threatens him with lynching. While Curley's wife is trapped in similar mental and physical prisons enforced by those in power, she has chosen this life for herself, marrying Curley to spite her mother; Crooks, meanwhile, is forced into his miserable life by societal forces beyond his control and has no plausible way to escape his situation.

Steinbeck also takes care to show us that Crooks' wasted potential is perhaps the greatest of all the characters. As an intellectual with 'gold-rimmed spectacles', Crooks has virtually no chance to manifest his ambitions. This futility is shown by the pathetic collection of his library:

the 'California civil code for 1905' and a 'tattered dictionary'. Crooks, then, is the only character who is not born to the farm; unlike a character such as Slim, who can make the most of his physical gifts, Crook's intellectual potential is marginalised to the point of invisibility. His inability to strive for improvement in his condition is further evidenced in the imaginative salvation of the ranch that George, Lennie and Candy are going to purchase. While Crooks is permitted a brief reverie in which he imagines himself as a participant in the shared dream of the other three men, he eventually realises that it is one that will not realistically come true for him, as he tells Candy to 'forget' what he said about 'hoein' and doin' odd jobs'. Even before the other three are forced to acknowledge the impossible nature of their dream in the most traumatic terms, Crooks leaves the shared picture as soon as he enters it, again reduced to a lonely figure 'rubbing his back'.

Although all of the characters in *Of Mice and Men* live in bleak conditions, Crooks' situation can be seen as the bleakest among the entire cast of characters. As the most isolated figure in the novella, Crooks' enforced insularity is a curse that is only temporarily lifted before being thrust back again. The scars he carries from a lifetime of exclusion and rejection, as well as his inability to live up to his intellectual potential, further confirm the desolate and miserable situation in which this relatively minor character finds himself.

REFERENCES & READING

Text

Steinbeck, J 2000, *Of Mice and Men,* Penguin Books, London. First published in 1937.

Other sources

Arbeiter, M 2017, '15 things you might not know about *Of Mice and Men*', *Mental Floss*, 27 Feb, www.mentalfloss.com/article/64095/15-things-you-might-not-know-about-mice-and-men

Bragg, M 2011, 'John Steinbeck's bitter fruit', *The Guardian,* 22 November, https://www.theguardian.com/books/2011/nov/21/melvyn-bragg-on-john-steinbeck

Gilmore, A 2001, 'John Steinbeck', *The Expository Times* 112 (6), 1 March, pp.192–6.

Howard, S 2020, 'Herbert Hoover and the 1930 drought', *National Archives*, 16 Sep, https://hoover.blogs.archives.gov/2020/09/16/herbert-hoover-and-the-1930-drought/

Lawrence, C 2020, 'Is Lennie a monster? A reconsideration of Steinbeck's *Of Mice and Men* in a 21st century inclusive classroom context', *Palgrave Communications* 6 (17), 31 Jan, https://www.nature.com/articles/s41599-020-0393-8

Lea, R 2015, 'Idaho parents push for schools to ban *Of Mice and Men* for its "profanities"', *The Guardian*, 8 May, https://www.theguardian.com/books/2015/may/07/idaho-parents-profane-of-mice-and-men-banned-schools-john-steinbeck

Parini, J 1994, *John Steinbeck: A biography*, Henry Holt, New York.

Shannon, P 1994, 'The long retreat of John Steinbeck', *Green Left*, 20 July, https://www.greenleft.org.au/content/long-retreat-john-steinbeck

Shiller, R 2017, 'The transformation of the American dream', *The New York Times*, 4 Aug, https://www.nytimes.com/2017/08/04/upshot/the-transformation-of-the-american-dream.html

Stancliff, D 2013, 'Remembering John Steinbeck, a great American writer', *Times Standard*, 24 Feb, https://www.times-standard.com/2013/02/24/remembering-john-steinbeck-a-great-american-writer/

Steinbeck, J 1960, 'A primer on the 30s', *Esquire*, 1 Jun, https://classic.esquire.com/article/1960/6/1/a-primer-on-the-30s

Swancutt, K 2019, 'Animism', *The Cambridge Encyclopedia of Anthropology*, 25 Jun, https://www.anthroencyclopedia.com/entry/animism